MIDDLEMARCH

THOMAS A. DUFF
ASSISTANT PROFESSOR OF ENGLISH
SETON HALL UNIVERSITY

Simon & Schuster, Inc.
15 Columbus Circle
New York, NY 10023

Copyright © 1965 by
Simon & Schuster

ISBN: 0-671-00709-2

Library of Congress Catalog Card Number: 66-1887

Printed in the United States of America

CONTENTS

INTRODUCTION

SOCIAL BACKGROUND: Revolution was the key word of nineteenth-century Europe. It was the age of industrial revolution, of scientific upheaval culminating in Charles Darwin's *Origin of Species,* of political transformations brought on by the appeals of nationalism, liberalism and—at length—socialism. Although it escaped the violence and bloodshed that attended the change in the Continent, Britain emerged triumphant from the Napoleonic wars, and faced a series of economic and social crises. These years, the years of maturity for George Eliot (1819–1880), and the period of the narrative in *Middlemarch,* saw indignant and ultimately successful protests against a political system which, even in its most democratic branch, the House of Commons, permitted less than one-sixth of the adult male population to vote.

NEED FOR REFORM: The great mass of English workers lived in appalling misery and degradation—there was much truth in Napoleon's remark that the British ruling classes treated the rabble like slaves. A typical skilled textile-worker received eighty shillings for a ninety-hour, six-day week. And those who were employed were the lucky ones. Hundreds of thousands of unemployed workers lived in abject poverty in the slums of "machine-age" cities like Birmingham and Leeds. Many of these were displaced farmers driven from their lands by the Enclosures Acts. Although successful in putting English agriculture on a more efficient basis, and perhaps necessary to feed a growing population, this legislation increased an already swollen labor market and aggravated the misery of the workers. Conditions in factory towns were intolerable, but the proponents of reform, such as the Scottish industrialist Robert Owen or the clergyman Charles Kingsley, encountered a cold hostility from the gentry, who took comfort in the dismal dogmas of classical economists like Thomas Malthus, David Ricardo, and others preaching the futility of any attempt to alleviate poverty.

REFORM BILLS: These were the five measures which liberalized representation in the House of Commons. Prior to the first, the Reform Bill of 1832, representation in Parliament was based

5

on a system dating from Queen Elizabeth I's reign (1558–1603), which failed to allow for shifts in population or the formation of new classes of society which followed in the wake of the Industrial Revolution. Two major abuses of the restrictions upon the franchise were:

1. "Pocket boroughs": those voting districts which were under the control of either the crown or of a large landholder.

2. "Rotten boroughs": those in which population had declined and whose power had fallen under the control of narrow town oligarchies or local landowners.

Each "pocket" or "rotten" borough, however, sent two members to Parliament; yet the large manufacturing cities such as Manchester and Birmingham were unrepresented. Of the total British population in 1831, consisting of twenty-four million people, only four hundred thousand were eligible to vote. Widespread corruption and the sale of parliamentary seats flourished, until dissatisfaction led to government action.

REFORM BILL OF 1832:   Enacted under the Whig administration of Lord Grey, this first of five reform bills (the others were in 1867, 1884, 1918, and 1928) was far from perfect, but certain positive measures had been taken to adjust the inequity of the franchise:

1. Seats were redistributed, an action which thereby improved the power of the larger cities and towns.

2. In the boroughs, any person who occupied premises with an annual value of ten pounds received the franchise.

3. In the counties, any leaseholder who occupied premises with an annual value of ten pounds received the franchise.

4. Voter registration and voting procedure were simplified.

With the passage of the first Reform Bill over eight hundred thousand Englishmen were finally permitted to vote.

CHARTISM: In English reform movements, "Chartism" is the name given to the period of 1838–1848. The Reform Bill of 1832 failed to extend the franchise to the poorer classes; this fact, and a widespread discontent with economic deprivation, brought about widespread approval, in 1838, of the "People's Charter." Written by William Lovett and Francis Place, the document advocated the following:

1. Universal manhood suffrage.
2. Voting by secret ballot.
3. Election of Parliament annually.
4. Removal of property qualifications for the House of Commons.
5. Payment of salary for members of the House of Commons.
6. Formation of equal voting districts.

The movement, which had the support of many trade unions, represented the first attempt by the English working classes to win political power. Although a number of parliamentary reforms were begun under the Chartist activities, its force died out because of civil strife between moderate and extremist factions within the movement.

RATIONALISM: In religion, rationalism is the philosophical view which believes as true only those tenets of religious belief which can be established by reason. Supernatural revelation and the mysteries of faith are generally denied. Although the orthodox positions of formal religious faiths are found to be unacceptable by rationalistic standards, many individual rationalists find a positive force, an "Unseen Divinity," operating in the world. Others, however, deny the existence of a supreme being, and consider the most worthy reward one can expect for leading a good life is the life itself, and the hope that future generations of mankind will profit from it.

LIFE: In 1857, a middle-aged English woman upon the advice of her husband assumed the pen name of George Eliot and began to publish fiction. Two of her most popular novels, *Silas Marner* and *Middlemarch,* are widely read today, and her repu-

tation as a major chronicler of English village life has endured
for over a century.

Mary Ann (or Marian) Evans was born on November 22, 1819,
at South Farm, Nuneaton (near Coventry), in Warwickshire,
England. Her father, like Caleb Garth in *Middlemarch,* was
an estate manager for several squires. He had five children,
three by an earlier marriage. Mary Ann attended good boarding
schools and excelled in language study until she was forced to
return to supervise the family upon the death of her mother
and the marriage of her sister (at which time she changed her
name from Mary Ann to Marian).

Her love for language, however, did not cease; she continued
her studies of German and Italian and also began the study of
Hebrew. When she was twenty-two, the family moved to Coventry; here Mary Ann met and was influenced by the anti-
Christian philosophy of Charles Hennell and Charles Bray and
his wife. It was shortly thereafter that she renounced her
Evangelical (Anglican) beliefs. Although she continued to respect the viewpoint of churchgoers, she remained a skeptic until her death. Her father (who had been distressed by his
daughter's loss of faith) died in 1849. This was three years
after Marian had published a translation of the erudite German
work, *The Life of Jesus (Das Leben Jesu),* an unorthodox view
of Christ which denied the supernatural elements in the Gospels.

After her father's death, she went abroad for eighteen months,
returning home in 1851 to accept a post as assistant editor with
The Westminster Review. Living in the London building which
housed the magazine offices, she soon became immersed in a
stimulating intellectual circle. It included the brilliant philosopher Thomas Carlyle, and the critic and editor George Henry
Lewes. Marian's wan complexion, large equine features, and
serious demeanor contrasted with the depth and acuity of her
mind and the brilliance of her conversation. Lewes had a broken
complexion and was extremely short, but he was witty, urbane,
and a versatile writer. When they met, Lewes' wife had recently
deserted him and their three children; Marian Evans and he,
defying convention, soon formed an attachment in which she
accepted the role of wife, but without legal contract. The couple

left immediately for a tour of Germany. Upon their return to London, many (but not all) of their free-thinking London friends accepted their action as a logical consequence of rationalistic beliefs. A great irony for many readers of Eliot's novels is the disparity between the consistent didacticism throughout her writing and the irregularity of her relationship with Lewes.

In 1857, at the urging of Lewes, she began to publish serially her first short stories and sketches under the pseudonym of George Eliot. (Notice Lewes' first name and the similarity between "Evans" and "Eliot.") The chronology of her work covers almost twenty years. *Scenes of Clerical Life* appeared in 1858. It is a work comprising three stories: "The Sad Fortunes of the Reverend Amos Barton," "Mr. Gilfil's Love Story," and "Janet's Repentance." Her first novel, *Adam Bede,* appeared in 1859 and was followed by *The Mill on the Floss* in 1860 and *Silas Marner* in 1861. These four titles form the body of her first period of work, based on the memories of her youth in Warwickshire. To many readers, her later novels fail to capture the imagination of these early ones, set in the rustic English countryside. Virginia Woolf, the twentieth-century novelist and critic, suggests that George Eliot is out of her element when she leaves the rustic scenes to portray higher levels of society. In *The Common Reader* Mrs. Woolf observes: "She is in the first place driven beyond the home world she knew and loved and forced to set foot in middle-class drawing rooms where young men sing all the summer morning and young women sit embroidering smoking-caps for bazaars. She feels herself out of her element, as her clumsy satire of what she calls 'good society' proves."

The middle period of her work includes *Romola,* a historical novel set in Florence, and *Felix Holt,* a political novel set in England during the era of the first Reform Bill. Her later period embraces *Middlemarch* (1871), a complex treatment of provincial life on its various levels. This novel, first published serially, is considered by many critics to be her masterpiece. Her final novel, *Daniel Deronda* (1876), presents a positive picture of Jewish life, perhaps the finest ever painted by a Christian author.

George Henry Lewes died in 1878. In November of the same year George Eliot published a book of essays called *The Impressions of Theophrastus Such,* probably written before Lewes' death. George Eliot died two years later on December 22, 1880, a few months after marrying John W. Cross, who was her official biographer. Arranged by form, her major works include:

TRANSLATIONS

1846   *Life of Jesus* by David Friedrich Strauss
1854   *Essence of Christianity* by Ludwig Andreas Feuerbach

POEMS

1868   *The Spanish Gypsy*
1874   *Jubal and Other Poems*

NOVELS

1858   *Scenes of Clerical Life*
1859   *Adam Bede*
1860   *The Mill on the Floss*
1861   *Silas Marner*
1863   *Romola*
1866   *Felix Holt the Radical*
1871   *Middlemarch*
1876   *Daniel Deronda*

ESSAYS

1879   *Impressions of Theophrastus Such*

CAREER: George Eliot, in the opinion of David Cecil, a modern critic of the Victorian novel, is the "first modern novelist." The first period of the English novel, he suggests, begins with Henry Fielding and ends with Anthony Trollope; the second, the period of Henry James, George Meredith, John Galsworthy and H. G. Wells, begins with George Eliot. Her art was intellectual; it was inspired by what she thought, and she used the novel to express her judgments on life. Her characters and scenes are secondary to her aim in fiction: the expression of a theme. She avoided the pat, happy endings of earlier novelists, if the logical working out of a character's situation demanded a tragic ending. Eliot, then, is a serious and moral novelist whose chief standard for judging people was based on the extent of their dedication to a life purpose. Her altruism is expressed in her writing goals: "My artistic purpose," she said, "is to present mixed human beings in such a way as to call forth tolerant judgment, pity and sympathy."

Her art ranges upon subjects taken from upper, middle, and the lower classes of small English towns or villages. The characterizations show careful research, indicative of the worth the author placed upon industry, restraint, and conscientiousness. Gradual development of character absorbs her—and is probably her most obvious forte. Basic changes which a character undergoes are carefully plotted and explained; we observe detailed, reflective explorations in the thinking of the characters of her novels. Usually a major character is confronted with a moral choice; he lives in a responsible world in which ethical values are strong; no acts are excused because a person is reduced merely to responding to an environment which determines what he will choose. The failure to live wisely is ultimately punished; secret remorse, if not public censure, functions as a nemesis for foolish or evil actions. Perhaps this poetic justice is at times unduly severe: to some the fate of John Raffles may appear capricious. To others, the somber tone of George Eliot's morality is supposedly relieved by the warm, simple humor of lower-class talk and gossip. Reserved for tavern and clerical characters and other "acceptable" types, it is quaint but hardly provoking.

DETAILED SUMMARY

PRELUDE

From rugged Avila, a Spanish town, St. Theresa ventured forth one day into the fearful land of the Moors. The innocent little girl and her younger brother had left to sow goodness and gain martyrdom—and both were stopped by their uncles.

> **COMMENT:** One of the basic themes of *Middlemarch* is the disparity between one's idealistic goals and the difficulties which life provides to thwart them. St. Theresa and her brother represent idealism; their uncles symbolize reality.

It was an appropriate beginning for a child destined to become one of history's great women. The fuel that nourished the fire burning within her drove her to seek infinite satisfaction, the perfect good, a goal which could satisfy and justify a moral life, yet one of action as well as meditation. She attained her goal in the reform of a religious order.

> **COMMENT:** There are many women born with spiritual grandeur similar to the Saint of Spain, but whose lives are unhistoric and uneventful on a grand scale. Their lives are filled with frustration, mistakes, and failure; their natures struggle against the barriers which society and circumstance impose. Because of the ardor they possess and the era and circumstances into which they are born, they are destined to be misunderstood, slandered, and ridiculed. Their ideals, although noble and well intentioned, are out of tune with the times and are considered eccentric. Such idealists are defeated by reality.

For the sake of clarity, George Eliot uses the brief prelude to state her theme: a universal conflict exists between individual growth and ambition in the face of adverse social or environmental conditions. Provincialism—of people devoted to material gratification and tolerant of culture only in its most super-

ficial forms—is the barrier which our protagonists, Dorothea
Brooke and Dr. Tertius Lydgate, must face. The intellectual and
social desires of the inhabitants of Middlemarch have little sympathy or understanding for such idealists. Incapable of high
aspirations themselves, Middlemarchers are inclined to allot
petty or ignoble motives to those whom they cannot readily
understand.

We are now about to be introduced to one of the finest panora-
mas of English provincial life in the early nineteenth century.
It is a time of complex social, economic, and political change,
which will leave England a more democratic country. It is, most
particularly, a time of reform, an appropriate atmosphere for
the rebellion of our characters against the general apathy of
their society.

BOOK ONE—MISS BROOKE

CHAPTER ONE

The time is 1829: the place is Tipton Grange, a village in England. As the novel opens, we are introduced to the Brooke sisters, Dorothea and Celia. Dorothea, nineteen, and the older by a year, has that quality of beauty which "plain fashion seems to enhance." (The Virgin Mary and the Bible are both used in her description, giving us a clue as to her spiritual character.) She has "contagious charm" and enjoys riding and the outdoors, but her puritan conscience and her energy are at odds. Dorothea is naïve, sympathetic, tender, magnanimous, and compulsive. Her sister Celia, on the other hand, is looked upon as the better prospect for marriage. She is amiable but practical, concerned more with outward appearances and impressions. She is, therefore, more "acceptable" by Middlemarch's provincial standards. Both are from an unquestionably "good" family, tracing back to the Puritans and Oliver Cromwell. Both their parents are dead; the girls are now staying at the country estate of their bachelor uncle, Mr. Arthur Brooke. He is a good-natured, foolish, and unpredictable gentleman of sixty-eight, whose grain of shrewdness makes him appealing and lovable. The sisters have inherited seven hundred pounds a year, and if Dorothea marries and has a son, he will inherit the Brooke estate. Dorothea, who is of a "theoretic" nature, yearns after "a lofty ideal," some principle which will justify her life and give meaning to her existence. The proper procedure for this quest, she believes, is to associate herself with some great man and assist him in bestowing his gifts for the benefit of mankind. She visualizes herself serving a man like John Milton or Thomas Hooker (profound English writers). Dorothea is entirely unaware of her attractiveness to the opposite sex and feels that all gentlemen visitors to the grange are in love with Celia. Dorothea's lofty ideals are looked upon by Middlemarch society as "peculiar," for conformity is the social and domestic temper of this society. Women are supposed to have weak opinions and passivity is given great value. Mr. Brooke is admonished continually by his social circle and by Mrs. Cadwallader, the rector's wife, in particular, for not having a middle-aged companion and guide for the girls.

The sisters are expecting two men for dinner that evening: Sir James Chettam, Dorothea's suitor, and Rev. Edward Causabon, a scholar of some reputation who is engaged in writing a long research work. During the day, Celia pleads with her sister to divide their mother's jewels, given to them by their uncle six months before. Dorothea is apathetic towards taking such worldly and superficial things but Celia energetically advances the following reasons for doing so.

Dorothea teases Celia, then relents, with a superior "Puritanic" tolerance. Celia has a placid nature that assents to her sister's sentiments but is never much disturbed by them. When viewing the jewels, Dorothea is reluctantly attracted to an emerald with diamonds (and in keeping with her spiritual nature compares it to the "spiritual emblems in the Revelation of St. John"). She keeps the emerald but suffers a pang of conscience when Celia intimates her inconsistency.

COMMENT: The first chapter of the novel introduces Dorothea Brooke to us. Clearly, she represents the idealistic and spiritual kind of woman whom Eliot describes in the Prelude. The differences between Dorothea and her sister Celia are noticed by the inhabitants of Middlemarch: to them Dorothea is an odd person because of her unusual values.

CHAPTER TWO

That evening at dinner, while Mr. Brooke discusses scientific farming and his acquaintances, Dorothea begins to form an impression of Reverend Casaubon. To her, he physically resembles the dignified and haunting portrait of John Locke, the English philosopher. She contrasts him with the vigorous Sir James Chettam. Mr. Brooke is opposed to the scientific approach to farming because it is too expensive and would lead to a complete reform. Dorothea argues that it would be to the good of the poor and the land. She idealistically states, "It is not a sin to make yourself poor in performing experiments for the good of all." Reverend Casaubon, who has been quietly observing, is impressed by Dorothea's energetic remark and fervor. After Mr. Brooke's generalizations on Adam Smith (an English economist) and Robert Southey (an English writer), Reverend Casaubon makes his first contribution to the conversation. We are informed that because of his research work on ancient times his eyes have been adversely affected, and so he must find someone to read for him. Reading has taken him much time, with the result that he has gotten "out of touch," so to speak: "I feed too much on the inward sources; I live too much with the dead."

Dorothea is much taken with Casaubon's learning and formality. She considers his attempt to reconstruct the past to be a very learned and noble venture. Here is the person she could associate herself with and help for the benefit of mankind. Mr. Brooke now discusses theology, Wilberforce (an English statesman and humanitarian) and the Catholic question (should Catholics be emancipated?), but Reverend Casaubon has been too busy with his studies to keep up on things. Brooke asks him how he keeps his documents organized. "In pigeon holes partly," replies Casaubon.

> **COMMENT:**   This reply gives us a suggestion of the narrowness and confinement of Casaubon.

Dorothea offers to organize her uncle's papers and Casaubon remarks that she would make a good "secretary."

Celia, discussing Casaubon in the drawing room, dislikes "the white moles" on his face; she also remarks that he is sallow; in general she considers him ugly and stuffy. Dorothea, or "Dodo" as Celia calls her sister, thinks he has a "great soul"; she reprimands Celia for judging a person by outward appearances only. Celia knows that Dorothea does not consider Sir James Chettam as a suitor, but he thinks she does. Much to her annoyance, Sir James continues to entreat Dorothea to give up horsemanship, until Casaubon intervenes by saying that Dorothea's motives must be respected and are no doubt of the highest merit. By forcing their revelation, they would tend to become less valuable. Sir James is forced to agree, but feels no jealousy since he believes Dorothea could not possibly be taken romantically with a "dried bookworm" of fifty like Casaubon. He then chats with Celia; when not near Dorothea, she talks freely. Sir James finds her amiable and pretty, although not superior to Dorothea.

CHAPTER THREE

The next morning, Dorothea continues her conversation with Reverend Casaubon, who is rector of Lowick (a town five miles from Tipton). He talks to her about the purpose of his work: to synthesize and find "A Key to All Mythologies" (the title of his work). To Dorothea, his ambitions and train of thought complement hers; subconsciously, she seeks a union with Casaubon. Because his research notes are voluminous he must condense them so that he can finally write and publish his work. The work, he reminds her, will take a great deal of time. Casaubon's explanation is delivered in a very scholarly and formal manner with very little emotion. Dorothea sees only what she wishes to see regarding Casaubon. She has faint stirrings that he can work to make her life "meaningful." She compares him to Jacques Bossuet (a French prelate, 1627–1704, author of *Discourse on Universal History,* 1681) and St. Augustine (the philosopher and theologian). Completely awed by his knowledge and understanding of the Ancients, she wishes to place her trust in him. Mr. Brooke persuades Casaubon to stay to view various documents and then to peruse his journal of travels. Casaubon politely tolerates him and is careful not to offend.

The next day Casaubon mentions to Dorothea that he has felt loneliness and the need of a youthful companion to lighten his "serious toils." This speech is made as if he were dictating a letter, it is so absent of feeling. After Casaubon leaves, Dorothea strolls in the woods, enjoying the autumnal loveliness. She contemplates her future with a man of such exalted purposes. She is very happy, although she realizes her idyllic love affair would be frowned upon by most young maidens of Middlemarch.

> **COMMENT:** Because she is so ardent, intellectual, and theoretical, Dorothea romantically imagines herself a sharer in Casaubon's great goal: the completion of his book. She looks to Casaubon to lead her out of the narrow confines imposed upon her by society and the dismal

passivity prescribed for women. He will "take her along the grandest path." She thinks his greatness will rub off on her.

She meets Sir James Chettam, whom she thinks is too patronizing. He remarks that he is envious of her power of forming an opinion, observing, "You seem to have the power of discrimination." He agrees to help Dorothea with her plans for building cottages for the workers on the estate. Perhaps she may be able to do the same at Lowick. Celia is sympathetic towards Sir James's illusion about Dorothea; she knows Dorothea is not impulsive and is amused at people who energetically express themselves.

> **COMMENT:**   Sir James' comment is ironic inasmuch as Dorothea's interest in Reverend Casaubon is hardly a "discriminating" one.

Casaubon now becomes a continual visitor, and Dorthea's first impressions of him are solidified. She likens his words to "a specimen from a mine, or the inscription on the door of a museum." She feels complimented when he appeals to her understanding or gives constructive criticism, but is disappointed when he shows lack of interest in her building plans. Mr. Brooke is invited to Lowick, and Dorothea and Sir James see each other often. She foresees a useful future for him with the right "feminine direction," and is most pleased that he is interested in her building plans.

> **COMMENT:**   Witness how Casaubon's words suggest a mine and a museum. Dorothea sees both as classical references; we view them as dark, ancient, and lifeless places. Objectively, Casaubon lacks real human impulses and warmth, but Dorothea's view of him clouds him in a romantic mist.

CHAPTER FOUR

Dorothea discovers from Celia that Sir James is in love with her and not her younger sister. This information is a product of gossip on the lower levels of Middlemarch society. Tantripp,

Brooke's maid, heard it from Sir James's man, who knew it from Mrs. Cadwallader's maid. Dorothea realizes now that she has recognized signs of his love; her revulsion is so great that tears well up in her eyes. She feels she must discontinue her plans for the cottages with him, a plan which the villagers think is just a fad, another one of Dorothea's peculiarities. She is very upset to think that others consider her useful and noble motive for the buildings to be fanciful. Mr. Brooke returns and comments upon the fresh air during his drive home. (This description is in contrast to Lowick with its stale air and oppressive and tomblike atmosphere.) Mr. Brooke thinks Casaubon is too deep in books saying, he "mopes, you know." He has known Casaubon for ten years and has witnessed nothing productive from him. Because of Dorothea's age (nineteen), Casaubon has asked Brooke for her hand. She accepts him, much to the surprise of Brooke, who wishes her to marry Sir James. He tells Dorothea that Casaubon is not young and warns her that his health is weak, but he will not interfere. Dorothea's wish is to have a husband who is more profound than she, one who will show her "right opinions" and their ultimate value, so that she can build her life on them.

Mr. Brooke thinks he has presented the disadvantages of such a marriage to his niece; yet he recognizes that Casaubon's scholarly ways may suit her. Women are inconsistent anyway, and always a problem. He shrugs his shoulders, with the thought: "To judge what sort of marriage would turn out well for a young girl who prefers Casaubon to Chettam" is pure folly.

COMMENT: Dorothea's decision to marry Casaubon follows soon after her rejection of Sir James's offer of marriage. We see the pressure of a provincial social conscience brought to bear upon an altruistic person in the suffering Dorothea experiences when she learns of the townspeople's reaction to her building plans.

CHAPTER FIVE

The chapter opens with a letter which Reverend Casaubon has written as a marriage proposal to Dorothea. He gives an "accurate statement" of his feelings in inflated and pedantic prose.

Casaubon describes Dorothea "as that rare combination of elements." He gives reasons for marriage: "To supply aid in graver labours and to cast a charm over vacant hours." Dorothea is overwhelmed and grateful; now she will be able to grow intellectually and morally; she need no longer repress her ardent nature. She answers him immediately, seeing no reason to delay her reply. Dorothea frets about her penmanship, hoping to make a good impression on Casaubon. In her reply she expresses her utmost gratitude for the proposal and happily anticipates their marriage. Her uncle advises her to be cautious, giving a last plea for Sir James, but she is adamant. Brooke acquiesces with a speech on how scholarly pursuits interested him at one time. He knows also that Mrs. Cadwallader will have much to say to him.

> **COMMENT:** Notice how conscious of social criticism the people of Middlemarch are.

That evening, Celia supposes that Dorothea's agitated condition is caused by the disappointment over Sir James and the building plans. Before retiring, Dorothea tells Celia she is very happy; Celia thinks it is strange to go from one extreme to another. Casaubon is invited to dinner and Celia senses Dorothea's excitement when he accepts her invitation. Celia becomes a little alarmed when the thought crosses her mind that Casaubon might mean something serious to "Dodo." Dorothea (in a pensive mood now) is debating whether to tell Celia of their engagement. Celia begins to ridicule Reverend Casaubon's foibles: he scrapes his spoon in his soup bowl and blinks before he speaks. It is then that Dorothea tells Celia of her engagement. Celia is shocked, but tenderness surmounts other feelings and she apologizes, wishing her sister happiness.

Dorothea still believes that Tipton criticizes her marriage. Upon seeing Casaubon later that evening, she pledges herself to him and he is flattered. She begs him to show her how she may best serve him to further all his great ends. Casaubon considers her "ardent self-sacrificing affection" to be an admirable quality. His frigid rhetoric is supplied with warmth and sincerity by Dorothea's sympathetic but limited point of view. They find themselves happy together and decide to marry within six weeks.

> **COMMENT:** Dorothea has now practically sealed her

avenues of escape. Her "theoretical" nature is composed both of genuine innocence of the ways of the world and of a kind of moral shortsightedness which mistakes prison for liberty.

CHAPTER SIX

Mrs. Cadwallader, wife of the rector of Tipton and Freshitt, passes Casaubon on her way to visit Mr. Brooke. She stops to gossip and bargain with the lodgekeeper about poultry. Mrs. Cadwallader is of "immeasurably" high birth and known to the farmers and laborers of that area as an inquisitive, witty, and sharp woman who "pleaded" poverty, and "pared down" prices. However, if anyone were to get too familiar, she would remind them of who she was. She often chides Brooke about entertaining Casaubon and threatens to expose him as a Whig and a Catholic Bill sympathizer; she also warns him against running for office as an independent. Known as a "matchmaker," she is very surprised when Brooke tells her that Dorothea will not marry Sir James, who is Mrs. Cadwallader's choice. When questioned as to whom she will marry, Mr. Brooke makes a hasty exit, to avoid the sharp tongue of the rector's wife. He leaves this unpleasant task to Celia. Mrs. Cadwallader thinks the whole affair is "frightful" but knows it had to be Dorothea's idea. She will now devote her talents to uniting Celia and Sir James. When she informs Sir James of the impending marriage, he expresses disgust and compares Casaubon to a mummy. They know Brooke will never be talked into disapproving the match. Before Mrs. Cadwallader leaves, she advises Sir James that Celia is impressed with him. He resolves to ride to Tipton Grange because he wants to meet the challenge of being a "good sport" about the intended marriage and because he knows Celia will be there, a thought which makes him feel better about the situation.

COMMENT: Mrs. Cadwallader is a familiar figure in literature: the solicitous matron whose chief vocation is to determine which unsuspecting men and women she can manage to manipulate into marriage. Such flabby cupids, soaring with arrows poised, shall, like lovers, always be with us.

CHAPTER SEVEN

In the time prior to the marriage, Reverend Casaubon visits the Grange often. He has deliberately put aside his research to relax and enjoy Dorothea's companionship. He finds his stream of desire quite shallow and thinks the poets exaggerate the "force of masculine passion." He cannot find the cause of his lack of ardor in any deficiency of Dorothea. She expresses a wish to learn Latin and Greek so that she may be of greater assistance to him and to develop her range of knowledge. She has a selfish motive also because she feels this "realm of masculine scholarship" may hold the "core of things": armed with learning she may be able to interpret correctly the social duties of a Christian. Casaubon consents reluctantly to instruct Dorothea. He finds it disagreeable and is unable to answer her questions intelligently, but it is Dorothea who feels that *she* lacks the intellectual depth for such an endeavor. Mr. Brooke, of course, agrees with her. He feels such profound studies as the classics and mathematics are too taxing for any woman. Dorothea would be "better employed" studying music. (She knows little about that art because at this time it was discouraged.) Casaubon can only tolerate with moderation "grander forms of music worthy to accompany solemn celebrations." He can accept only those forms approved by ancient conception. Mr. Brooke regards Dorothea's hopes as "unhealthy" and instructs Casaubon to have a quieting influence on his niece. He thinks Casaubon is affluent, and a sensible person; perhaps some day he may even become a dean or a bishop.

> **COMMENT:**   Observe how Eliot gradually cracks the plaster of the saint Dorothea imagines Casaubon to be.

CHAPTER EIGHT

In this chapter, we are concerned primarily with Sir James's attempts to prevent the match. He finds it easier now to visit the Grange after his initial encounter with Dorothea. He feels no jealousy toward Casaubon, but is shocked that Dorothea labors under this "melancholy illusion." Sir James, convinced that Mr. Brooke should have prevented the match, visits rector Cadwallader (who is a good friend), and asks him to intervene on the grounds that Dorothea is not of age. At first, the rector thinks that Sir James wants him to stop Brooke from running for office on the Whig ticket. (The rector's remark is indicative of the general feeling towards Brooke's political aspirations.) Anyone who is anti-Whig should be very happy when the Whigs fail to select the strongest candidate to run. He soon realizes that the visit is not for this purpose. Sir James tells the rector that both he and Celia have judged Casaubon alike; he remarks, "He is fifty and he never could have been much of a man." When the rector asks the reasons for Chettam's dislike, Sir James is stunned to think that the rector is not in sympathy with him. He asks, "Has he got any heart?" The rector proceeds to tell of Casaubon's fair and just treatment of his relatives. Sir James is still unconvinced, informing Cadwallader that his motive for trying to stop the marriage is simply because he believes that Dorothea will suffer for it.

Mrs. Cadwallader enters with her young son; she tells Sir James that she and her husband have "washed their hands" of the affair. One last plea is made by Sir James but it is repulsed by the rector. He feels that Casaubon has done his duty to his profession, has done no visible harm to anyone and, finally, that he apparently loves Dorothea.

Afterwards, Sir James, maintaining his good disposition, continues to help Dorothea with her cottages, enjoying her company even more now that there is no "passion to hide or confess."

CHAPTER NINE

Dorothea wishes to see her new home at Lowick to make any changes necessary.

> **COMMENT:** George Eliot's humorous maxim is appropriate here: "A woman dictates before marriage in order that she may have an appetite for submission afterwards."

Dorothea travels to Lowick with her uncle and Celia, who does not fail to point out the depressing aspects of the manor house at Lowick. It is an old-fashioned house; on this gray November morning the southern and eastern parts of the house appear "rather melancholy": the grounds are more confining and the flower beds need tending. The manor is small-windowed and has an air of "autumnal decline." It is a home which needs flowers, children, and open windows to make it livable. Dorothea sees great possibilities and imagines the house to be "hallowed."

> **COMMENT:**　　To Dorothea, the dark bookshelves and faded curtains and carpets have been subdued by time. An old vase here and there and curious old maps and other images help to suggest how depressing Reverend Casaubon is, for the house is a reflection of his personality.

Dorothea sees no changes to be made. Casaubon inquires as to which room she would prefer. She has no favorite but Celia does, and Mr. Brooke comments that the bow-windowed room would be nice after some alterations. Dorothea wants no changes. Mr. Casaubon points out his aunt among a group of miniatures in the room, but tells Dorothea little about her other than that she had an unfortunate marriage. Celia, in an aside, tells her sister that she recently saw a young man (Will Ladislaw), who physically resembled Casaubon's aunt. They then meet Mr. Tucker, the curate (a minor clergyman). He is unfavorable in Celia's eyes because the "corners of his mouth are so unpleasant." She dreads the time she must spent as bridesmaid at Lowick. Mr. Tucker answers Dorothea's questions, but she is disappointed that the people of the village appear well and satisfied, because now there is nothing she can do for them. She then makes a mental note to devote more time to Casaubon's aims.

In the garden of the manor house, Dorothea meets the young man whom Celia had mentioned as resembling Casaubon's aunt. He is Will Ladislaw, Casaubon's second cousin and the grandson of his Aunt Julia. She looks at the sketches he is drawing and makes an innocent comment which he misunderstands as criticism. Ladislaw thinks Dorothea must be unpleasant and certainly can have no passion if she is to marry Casaubon. We learn from Casaubon that Ladislaw attended Rugby but refused to go to an English university. It was his choice to study at Heidelberg. He now wants to go abroad for "cultural preparation."

COMMENT: From this first impression we may consider Will Ladislaw to be unsettled; Eliot depicts him as a "dabbler" in the arts, a reformer, and a freethinker.

Casaubon is supporting Will and is paying for his education. He has tried to give Will a sense of responsibility and discipline, feeling they are necessary prerequisites for a life's vocation. He underscores that his own manuscript is the result of hard work, discipline, and preparation for a work not yet accomplished. Dorothea thinks Casaubon to be very noble for having patience with young Ladislaw by continuing to support and guide him.

COMMENT: One suspects that Will has a better understanding of Casaubon than Casaubon has of him.

CHAPTER TEN

Will decides not to fix his European destination any more precisely than the "Continent." He feels that genius must not be confined but must have the opportunity to receive its motivation from a wide number of stimuli. He has drunk wine excessively and has experimented with opium to see what effects they would have on his creativity. Nothing original resulted from these measures. He thinks it is only a matter of time before his genius will evolve. He feels Casaubon's impotence with his work to be no example to follow.

COMMENT: Eliot now shifts her attention to Casaubon. She makes a plea for tolerance for him, suggesting that anyone would have come in for their share of criticism from Mrs. Cadwallader, Mr. Brooke, Sir James, and Celia. Certainly, in spite of Casaubon's rigid method of discourse and his unimpassioned nature, we should not imagine he has no feeling or good work in him at all.

Naturally enough, Casaubon considers himself to be the center of his universe. He is touched by thoughts of his forthcoming marriage, but is surprised to find that his spirit is not rising; he is disappointed because he is not more enchanted by romance. Inasmuch as he had restrained his emotions and rationed his affection, he thought he would now have an abundance to use.

He finds he is more barren of sensibilities at the very time they should be most ripe. Utterly alone and despairing, he fears he is endlessly toiling—sifting his mass of notes—yet getting no closer to his goal.

Dorothea, on the other hand, is looking forward to marriage with great expectations. It will open new vistas of learning for her. It is decided that Rome is to be the destination of the wedding trip. Casaubon suggests a traveling companion for Dorothea since he will be very busy doing research in culturally rich Rome. Dorothea is hurt, not so much because Casaubon may neglect her on their honeymoon, but because he shuns her help in his research.

There is a party at the Grange, the last preliminary preparation for the wedding. Dorothea is the subject of many observations this evening. Some of the guests include the newly elected mayor of Middlemarch (Mr. Vincy), who "happened to be a manufacturer," and his brother-in-law the philanthropic banker, Mr. Bulstrode, who is called by different names by the townspeople ("hypocrite," "Methodist dissenter"). Before reform took hold there was a clearer distinction of class in Middlemarch, and this party was considered too "miscellaneous" for many of the people. The variety of guests is the product of Mr. Brooke's liberal leanings and "inordinate travel." At the party, several of the men discuss their preferences in women. Mr. Chichely, a middle-aged bachelor, indicates his preference for flirtatious, coquettish women. He holds up the mayor's daughter, Rosamond Vincy, as an example of an ideal woman. The women at the party make fun of Casaubon's "drying up of passion"; they judge Dorothea to be excessively "earnest." We are introduced to Dr. Lydgate in the women's conversation. They describe him to be clever and a gentleman with a "fine brow."

> **COMMENT:**   Dr. Lydgate, one of the novel's major figures, is indeed a gentleman. He comes from a good background, which was quite unusual for medical men at that time. The profession was mistrusted, misunderstood, and was considered to be one of the lesser vocations for gentlemen.

Lydgate is reputed to be treating fever in a way different from the usual manner. He makes a good impression on Lady Chettam because he neither agrees or disagrees with her. A very clever conversationalist, he never offends. He has studied in Paris, where he met outstanding men, and he has ideas for raising the standards of the medical profession. Lydgate is unimpressed when he meets Dorothea.

Soon after the party, the marriage takes place and the Reverend and Mrs. Casaubon leave for Rome on their wedding trip.

> **COMMENT:**   Witness how Eliot captures the life of Middlemarch by presenting social situations. In this instance, she shows us a prewedding party, complete with its gallery of character types and gossip.

> At this point in the novel the attention will shift from Dorothea Brooke to Dr. Lydgate. Eliot introduces us to him in this transitional chapter because succeeding chapters will be concerned with his fortunes. A second plot, then, is about to begin.

CHAPTER ELEVEN

Dr. Lydgate is very much attracted to a young girl noticeably different from Dorothea Brooke: Rosamond Vincy. Anxious to start his medical practice, he feels that love and marriage are impractical until he becomes firmly established in his profession. To Lydgate, Dorothea is too inquisitive, opinionated, and moralistic.

> **COMMENT:**   Lydgate's error here is that he is unable to see deeper into a person's character.

His ambition is to reform the medical profession of his time, and such a hope is not conducive to getting rich quickly. Wealth, however, is secondary to Lydgate. Rosamond was the pride of Mrs. Lemon's school, a sort of finishing school for girls who sought to acquire the social graces. Lydgate is attracted by the superficial characteristics of Rosamond. The Vincy family is socially prominent: Mr. Vincy's sister Harriet married the wealthy, influential banker, Nicholas Bulstrode, who was considered to have improved himself by this marriage. Mr. Vincy

married an innkeeper's daughter and Mrs. Vincy's sister was
the second wife to rich old Mr. Featherstone, but she had died
childless years ago. Lydgate inherits Mr. Featherstone and Bulstrode as patients. Rosamond wishes her father would employ
Dr. Lydgate since she is bored with the local young men; a
stranger would be an exciting diversion. She has no patience
with her brothers, especially Fred, whose father is anxious for
him to take a degree and become a minister. Fred is opposed
to such a future and spends his time in the pursuit of pleasure,
much to the consternation of his good-natured mother. Rosamond and Fred tease each other constantly. She considers it a
disadvantage to have been born a daughter of a Middlemarch
manufacturer and is ashamed that her mother was the daughter
of an innkeeper. Her mother wanted Rosamond to go to Featherstone's home "Stone Court" when Mrs. Vincy's sister died, but
she refused. A girl named Mary Garth now attends to Mr.
Featherstone's needs, and there is a fear that she will inherit
some of his money. Fred informs Rosamond that their uncle is
ill and that he is going to visit him, when Dr. Lydgate goes to
attend him. Rosamond looks upon the visit as an opportunity
to meet the new doctor; she decides to go along with Fred.

CHAPTER TWELVE

The wealthy Peter Featherstone is very seriously ill and is visited by his sister, Mrs. Waule, at Stone Court in Lowick parish.
Wealthy in her own right, she has fear of anyone other than the
Featherstones inheriting her brother's money, and suggests to
him how unsteady his favorite nephew Fred is, with his constant gambling at billiards. She asserts that he has borrowed
a good deal of money on the strength of his inheritance when
Featherstone dies, a fact she has learned from her brother Solomon. She attempts to gain Featherstone's favor for his nephew
John on the Featherstone side of the family. Mrs. Waule is afraid
that Mary Garth will side with Fred in order to gain Featherstone's favor but Mary tells her she is not interested in any
scandal. When Fred and Rosamond arrive, Peter speaks alone
to his nephew, informing him of what he has just heard from his
sister. Fred denies the rumor (for he really had never borrowed
in this way). Featherstone mischievously hints that Bulstrode
was the informer and wishes Fred to solicit a letter from Bul-

strode stating that the banker has good faith in Fred's honor not to borrow money on the security of his (Featherstone's) land. This letter, Peter observes, will vindicate Fred. Fred has a problem, for he knows that Bulstrode, like other men, believes in rumors and that Bulstrode dislikes him. Fred appeals to his uncle's vanity by saying that the whole procedure is not gentlemanly. Peter has little use for Bulstrode, viewing him as a religious hypocrite, who is always fortifying his questionable dealings with a religious motive or justification. Good, solid land is God-given, but "speculating" is inspired by the devil, exclaims Peter. Peter promises to back Fred's debts "a bit" if the letter is delivered.

Rosamond and Mary, who had been lifelong acquaintances and attended the same provincial school, were enjoying their conversation. Mary, compared to Rosamond, appears very plain but has no illusions about life or herself. Shrewd and a little satirical, she is strong-willed and has a sense of obligation to her family. Mary is very receptive to sincerity but will not extend herself to those who "speak to me, without seeming to see me." She is in sympathy with Fred's rejection of the ministry but censors his aimlessness and idle ways. Rosamond's opinions appear superficial and vacant when compared with Mary's. Some of Rosamond's ideas about topics discussed during their brief chat are: (1) Love: interesting and agreeable people fall in love when in close proximity for any length of time. (2) Religion: it is a crutch to lean on when there are no other prospects in view. (3) Vocation: the vocation makes the man. Mary finds that Fred is in love with her but she will not marry him until he has matured and proven himself in some worthy vocation.

Dr. Lydgate arrives, a little disillusioned with Middlemarch charm and the prospect of his visit with Featherstone. Rosamond consciously dramatizes all her actions for the sole purpose of attracting Lydgate's favor. She succeeds admirably and when their eyes meet as he gives Rosamond her riding whip, she feels they have fallen in love! It had to happen this way, Rosamond contemplates, because she had constructed her future this way. On her way home she has reveries that Lydgate is in love with her; her brother Fred is meditating on his visit with his uncle; he knows that Featherstone enjoys tormenting him but does not realize that Peter had been teasing him about Bulstrode's informing him (Featherstone) of his debts. He hopes that his father will take upon himself the unpleasant task of speaking to Bulstrode.

BOOK TWO—OLD AND YOUNG

CHAPTER THIRTEEN

Mr. Bulstrode, the banker, is visited by Dr. Lydgate. Bulstrode wishes him to become superintendent of the new hospital which he is building in Middlemarch. Some men distrust Bulstrode because of his looks, his verbose speech, and his scrutiny of others in conversation. The villagers of Middlemarch are suspicious of his little-known past. Dr. Lydgate suggests a special wing for treatment of contagious diseases and has high hopes, after his reforms have taken hold, of starting a medical school. All his ideas are put forth in a confident manner and with a convincing mode of delivery. He has little regard for the obstacles to his ideas, but his good will saves him from being overbearing. Particularly impressed by the doctor because he is a stranger, Bulstrode cautions Lydgate about the possible jealousy of his fellow practitioners when they learn of his appointment as superintendent. Lydgate replies that he enjoys a good fight. Bulstrode now alludes to the spiritual condition of patients. He shows his political sense by suggesting that the doctor support Mr. Tyke over Mr. Farebrother for the paid position of chaplain at the hospital, although the proposed building stands in Mr. Farebrother's parish and he has been attending patients of the old hospital without compensation. Lydgate defers his judgment because a decision of this sort lies outside the realm of medical knowledge. Bulstrode then intimates that he has an ulterior financial motive for his interest in the affairs of the hospital. As Lydgate is leaving he meets and accepts a dinner invitation from Mr. Vincy, who has come in behalf of his son Fred. Mr. Bulstrode is quick to point out the errors of others and reprimands Vincy for his son's behavior; he suggests that it was not a spiritual motive but rather a worldly one which prompted Vincy to encourage his son to enter the clerical life. Vincy resents Bulstrode's superior attitude, especially in light of the prospect of his (Vincy's) becoming mayor, but he refrains from being argumentative. Mr. Vincy finally explains the purpose of his visit. Bulstrode suggests that he would not be surprised if the rumor of Fred's borrowing on the prospect of his uncle's death is true. Mr. Vincy argues that Fred would not lie to him or to anyone. Bulstrode thinks that by vindicating Fred and paving the way for his inheritance he will be doing Fred an injustice. "I cannot regard wealth as a blessing to those who use it simply as a harvest for this world." Vincy desperately attacks Bulstrode by suggesting that he is dishonest in one of his business partnerships: "Plymdale's house uses those blue and green dyes it gets from the Brassing manufactory; they rot the silk. . . ." Bulstrode assumes Vincy is taking advantage of his relationship as his brother-in-law. Vincy angrily tells Bulstrode that families should stick together and help one another; he warns Bulstrode that if he does not write the letter he (Vincy) will consider it "unhandsome and will not bear it well." He views a failure to support Fred's honor to be in fact spreading scandal about Fred. Bulstrode promises to consult his wife before making a decision.

> **COMMENT:** Bulstrode represents the author's view of a religious hypocrite, one who is most careful to maintain a spiritual exterior for business purposes, yet is quick to bend his ethical principles if personal gain may ensue.

CHAPTER FOURTEEN

The next day, Bulstrode writes the letter; Fred brings it to Peter Featherstone. It is very cleverly worded to absolve Fred of the rumor, yet it avoids any direct statements denying Fred's action. Old Featherstone is very disagreeable to Mary Garth since he has become ill. He enjoys taunting Fred about the monetary gift he is about to offer him. Much to Fred's disappointment the money he is given totals one hundred pounds, sixty less than his debt. Fred covers his disappointment and, when finally dismissed, seeks Mary.

In the conversation that ensues, we see the strong bond of the Garth family. Mary displays remarkable good judgment and common sense despite her strong feeling for Fred. Fred alludes to John Waule's love for her. Mary answers, "I have no ground for the nonsensical vanity of fancying everybody who comes near me is in love with me. I think any hardship is better than pretending to do what one is paid for, and never really doing it." Mary, goodnaturedly yet without any possibility of Fred's misunderstanding her meaning, reprimands him for his irresponsibility and debts. However, Fred is still very much impressed with the "higher education of the country," an impression which has distorted his respect of income and rank. He tries to get Mary to declare her love for him by saying a man can do nothing worthwhile unless he has the love of a woman. Mary thinks it would be an injustice to marry a man who is idle, although she might love him. Anyway, her father would not accept a shiftless man. She encourages him to pass his examinations but will promise him nothing. She cautions Fred never to speak to her of marriage and love again until he is gainfully employed. Fred is chagrined because it is Mary's father who is the signer of the bill which Fred owes to his creditor.

CHAPTER FIFTEEN

This chapter gives us background material about Dr. Lydgate and how he became interested in medicine. After attending public school he was orphaned and left in the care of guardians. He discovered an anatomy book by accident in his home library and soon dedicated himself to the study of medicine. He studied in London, Edinburgh, and Paris. In his youth, Lydgate was emotional, warm-hearted, and rash. He had a peculiar resistance to serious study, but was interested in human beings; he was a man as well as a doctor. He became attracted by the need for reform in the medical profession and judged the best opportunity for it and for serious medical work would be away from the city, in a provincial town where he could "win celebrity." Interested only in prescribing drugs (not dispensing them) and doing original work, Lydgate was fired with an ideal to become the perfect, dedicated doctor. He was ambitious to enlarge the scientific basis of his profession. At twenty-seven, Lydgate had become involved with an actress in Paris and offered to marry her through "impetuous folly" after she had been accused of killing her husband. To his sorrow, Lydgate discovered that she had meant to kill him out of hate; it was not chance, as he had believed. Disillusioned with women and determined to remain aloof, he had decided to settle down to a life of service and research in Middlemarch.

CHAPTER SIXTEEN

The question of appointing Mr. Tyke as hospital chaplain is an interesting topic to the people of Middlemarch. It indicates the power of the banker Mr. Bulstrode; he knows the financial secrets of most of the businessmen of the town since he administers the town charities. There are those who are openly opposed to him, and those who go the way the wind blows. Bulstrode willingly confers obligations, but is "severe" in watching the results. The more power he wins the better he learns to use it for the "glory of God." His "spiritual conflict" consists of adjusting his motives to harmonize with God's glory.

Mr. Vincy tells his dinner guest, Dr. Lydgate, that he favors Mr. Farebrother, who is a likeable person and who gives human and reasonable sermons, but he is opposed to Tyke because of his dogmatism (inflexible religious beliefs). Mr. Chichely, the coroner, wishes to have the directors and medical board decide the issue. Dr. Sprague (who has not kept up on medical changes) frowns upon the "foreign ideas" of Lydgate, who chooses to be outspoken and rash deliberately to encourage the disfavor of men like Chichely and Sprague.

At dinner, Lydgate and Rosamond become engrossed in conversation. She appears even more refined when compared to the unpretentiousness and "inoffensive vulgarity" of Mrs. Vincy. Rosamond is perfectly attuned to the social graces but lacks humor. She is an excellent singer and Lydgate is charmed. In short, he finds her utterly attractive and accomplished. Mr. Farebrother enters and soon extends an invitation to Lydgate to dine with him. He then proceeds to play a serious game of whist. Lydgate watches the game until eleven, when he leaves. He finds himself liking Farebrother, whose church is the oldest in Middlemarch and whose salary is barely enough to meet his needs. He next meditates on Rosamond, judging that when he is ready to marry in a few years he would like his wife to be like her: a girl who possesses intelligence, grace, and talents. Lydgate thinks that he is not likely to make the same mistake with Miss Vincy as he did with the Parisian actress. After all, he only "admires" Rosamond. At home, he decides to look into Louis' view on fever. Dr. Lydgate is happy in his work, not only for its intellectual content, but because of its involvement with human beings.

We leave his higher plane of thought to descend, somewhat, to Rosamond. She is not concerned with the state of mankind or with any occupation, but rather with a coquettish "inward repetition of looks, words and phrases." Rosamond sees no reason to delay her marriage plans, since she never questions whether Lydgate is in love with her. She vainly assumes that all men fall in love with her sooner or later. In her mind he is what she always dreamed of. He has all the necessary characteristics for her story-book romance.

COMMENT: The parallel between the budding love of Rosamond and Dr. Lydgate and the love of Dorothea and Casaubon is obvious. Both men view marriage somewhat reluctantly; the women view it romantically.

CHAPTER SEVENTEEN

Lydgate is invited to dine at the home of Mr. Farebrother. The house is old and dated. He lives with his mother, his aunt (Miss Noble), and Miss Winifred Farebrother, his older sister. His mother "was evidently accustomed to tell her company what they ought to think, and to regard no subject as quite safe without her steering." She informs Lydgate that they are not often in want of medical aid, since she is very careful in rearing her children.

Farebrother tells Lydgate that his ideals will not be easy to forward since the conservative Middlemarch society will fight him to preserve the status quo. Farebrother gives Lydgate good advice. With acute insight into human motives and acts, he tells him to keep himself independent of others, perfect his knowledge so people will realize his value, and choose a good wife—an unworldly woman. (He gives Miss Garth as a perfect example.)

Mr. Farebrother shows Dr. Lydgate his collection of nature-study specimens. Lydgate senses that this man of the cloth may have desired a different vocation. (Perhaps the dominance of his mother was responsible for his choice of the ministry over nature study.) Farebrother, who changes the topic from nature study, suggests that Lydgate avail himself of Bulstrode's favor and assistance by voting for Mr. Tyke as chaplain. He confides to Lydgate that they should remain friends, regardless of how he votes.

CHAPTER EIGHTEEN

Lydgate, who really has little interest in the question of the chaplaincy and who would have voted for Mr. Tyke out of convenience, is hesitant now because of his developing friendship with Mr. Farebrother. Lydgate admires his sacrificing of his own interest for his mother, sister and aunt; furthermore, his generosity and delicacy for Lydgate's situation are exemplary. Mr. Farebrother's character and conduct are unusually fine, and his sermons (delivered without a book), are attended by people outside his parish.

At Mr. Bulstrode's request, Dr. Lydgate is laying plans for the interior of the hospital. The voting has been given to the board of directors and the medical men; Lydgate knows he has to decide how to vote.

> **COMMENT:**   We see Lydgate faced with a possible loss of his independence if he succumbs to outside pressures; he realizes a vote for Tyke ensures an office for him, while a vote for Farebrother will result in the loss of the office.

Now Lydgate begins to rationalize his position and looks for faults in Farebrother: (1) He spends too much time on nonclerical occupations. (2) He plays cards for money. (3) He plays billiards frequently at the Green Dragon. (4) He probably does not care for the job but is more interested in the money. However, Lydgate thinks he can vote for Farebrother if there is no valid objection to him from anyone else, since he fears a vote for Tyke will make him a vassal of Bulstrode's. During the voting, Bulstrode becomes identified with Lydgate, and Lydgate with Tyke because of gossip begun by the doctors and the directors. Lydgate is not popular with medical men because

of his ideas on reform; in addition, they take it as an insult to
their standing because he has refused to "dispense" drugs. Bulstrode's enemies become Lydgate's, because of their alleged
friendship. The vote ends in a draw and Lydgate, when angered
by the remark of a Mr. Wrench that he is sure to vote the way
Bulstrode does, rashly *does* vote that way, the chaplaincy is
given to Mr. Tyke. Lydgate's conscience is troubled about this
for some time after.

> **COMMENT:**   The integrity of Lydgate is swayed by the
> pettiness of the Middlemarch doctors and his own emo-
> tion. One of the major themes in the novel is the conflict
> between idealists and the obstacles which reality places in
> their paths.

CHAPTER NINETEEN

In this chapter we return to the story of Dorothea and her husband, Rev. Casaubon. Will Ladislaw, traveling in Rome, learns
from a German artist (Adolf Naumann), of a woman of artistic
beauty he has seen in the museum, and whom he wants Will to
see. Much to Will's surprise, he discovers the woman is Dorothea. Adolf wishes to know if she is really married, since he
has mistaken Casaubon for her father! Will tells him that Casaubon is, indeed, her husband and that she is also his cousin.
Naumann wishes to paint her and expresses his desire to Will,
who becomes very much disturbed about the idea and at first
refuses. Naumann suggests the possibility of jealousy, which
Ladislaw rejects openly. Yet Will does have certain misgivings
about his motives; why did he object so strenuously to his
friend's proposed portrait of Dorothea?

> **COMMENT:**   Eliot's interest in the psychological aspects
> of a character is shown in the introspection Ladislaw un-
> dergoes concerning his possible jealousy.

CHAPTER TWENTY

We find Dorothea in her apartment in the Via Sistina, sobbing
bitterly. She has been in Rome five weeks and her puritanic con-
ceptions are blinding her to the city's treasures. She is content

only when she can be close to earth and sky—away from the "oppressive masquerade" of the ages. Casaubon spends little time with his melancholic bride. Her ardent nature, combined with English and Swiss puritanism make her view the culture of Rome in the light of irreverence and decay. She is thoroughly upset and lonely. To see the sensual and spiritual motifs of the Renaissance intermingled confuses her and checks her flow of responsive emotion.

> **COMMENT:** Casaubon, not Rome, is the cause of Dorothea's depression. Eliot uses Rome to suggest the disappointment Dorothea finds in her new husband.

Dorothea's view of her marriage is now beginning to change slightly although she is not aware of it. Casaubon only confuses her whenever she wishes to learn or to improve her understanding. She senses that she will never be able to aid him in his work. Casaubon lacks interest or sympathy in the face of the art and other great treasures of Rome; he seems fearful of committing himself to opinions, lest his superficial knowledge be discovered.

> **COMMENT:** Like Lydgate, Dorothea is warm and affectionate; had Casaubon at least responded accordingly she would have been content. Wtihout response, however, her suffering is acute.

Because of the turmoil inside her, Dorothea is disagreeable to Casaubon when he informs her that his study is not quite finished; although he has kept her away from Rome during the holidays he hopes that she is enjoying herself in his absence. He compliments her by saying that she has lightened his burden of thought when he is not studying. This remark is delivered with an absence of emotion or feeling, characteristic of his stylistically frigid, pedantic language. For the first time Dorothea asks him to make up his mind which notes of research he will use, and to begin to write the book and publish it. She pleads that she will do anything to help him attain this end. Her idea strikes a note of fear in Casaubon, because Dorothea may discover his lack of confidence in his ability to actually write the work. He becomes suspicious of her and is hurt by her perception of his pretenses to scholarship. Casaubon covers his stress by stating that he is an authority and knows when the book should be written; he tells Dorothea that she is incompetent to judge such a grand and profound undertaking. Dorothea then asks him why he never speaks of writing the work, instead of always discussing his row of notebooks!

To Dorothea's "ardent" nature, this first disagreement seems a catastrophe. To Casaubon, who already has been disappointed because of his lack of feeling during their marriage, Dorothea's plan is a new "pain"; he suffers in the knowledge that she is capable of hurting him cruelly. The couple drive to the Vatican in silence; when he departs, Naumann first glimpses her beside the statue. (Eliot uses the flashback technique here.)

> **COMMENT:**   Dorothea is now aware that her new husband is less of a warm, responsive person and more of a cold, disciplined note-taker than she had imagined.

CHAPTER TWENTY-ONE

Hurriedly drying her tears, Dorothea opens the door of the apartment to a visitor, Will Ladislaw. Aware of her husband's generosity toward Will, she hopes that she may now help her husband in his kind deeds. Casaubon is away for the whole day at the Vatican Library, feverishly filling his notebooks, for the Casaubons are soon to leave Rome. Privately, Will is annoyed with his cousin for leaving his new bride at home, alone, while he pursues his insignificant details elsewhere. Dorothea speaks of her confusion and negative feelings when viewing so many art treasures in Rome. In her simplicity, she tells Will to become an artist and to improve upon the great paintings of Rome; when he shows apathy towards such a vocation she chides him, like Casaubon does, for his lack of patience. Will states, "He and I differ." Dorothea, although she has just been reminiscing about her husband's tutorial manner and lack of warmth, speaks glowingly about his devotion to study. Such comments annoy Will, for he fails to understand how Dorothea can be so deceived by Casaubon. Much to her consternation, Will suggests that Casaubon's labors may be unnecessary because of the strides in research now being made by German historians. After his retort Will is contrite, because he feels he has hurt Dorothea's feelings.

He is very much impressed by her simplicity, generous feeling, and good nature and has a strong desire to help her understand Casaubon's false pretenses. Dorothea feels very responsive to Will and thanks him, thinking he understands her. She needs Will to talk to, to fill her lonely hours.

Casaubon enters and proceeds to exhibit all his usual dullness and formality. Even though he is unpleasantly surprised to find Will there, he never gives such an impression, remaining his imperturbable self. He invites Will to dinner the following evening. After Will leaves, Casaubon receives an apology from Dorothea for her disagreeable behavior at breakfast. Casaubon accepts it without much feeling and is tempted (by jealousy) to expose his dislike of meeting Will. Dorothea is now aware of her "wild illusion" of expecting a response from her husband; also, she discerns that there is a weakness in his character, which is in need of understanding on her part.

> **COMMENT:**   We witness Dorothea's attempts to adjust to her marriage. Although she is becoming aware of Casaubon's faults, Dorothea considers herself obliged to consider his feelings also.

CHAPTER TWENTY-TWO

Next evening at dinner, all is pleasant: the displeasure the Reverend Casaubon has experienced from his cousin's presence has been mollified and Will is ingratiatingly agreeable company. Dorothea and her husband even accept an invitation to accompany Will on a tour of artists' studios on the following day. Inevitably, they end their tour at Adolf Neumann's studio. Naumann is busily painting when they enter. His interest at present lies in spiritual and religious subjects, and he asks Casaubon to pose for the head of St. Thomas Aquinas. Casaubon is obviously flattered and allows Dorothea to pose for Santa Clara while he rests. He agrees to return the following day. Dorothea begins to feel differently about Rome and its treasures: she begins to feel exhilarated. Will is annoyed with Adolf when he rhapsodizes on Dorothea's beauty.

Will wants desperately to leave a lasting impression on Dorothea. He decides to visit her alone, without an invitation. Unaware of her husband's feeling about Will, Dorothea welcomes him enthusiastically, for she enjoys his company and thinks they complement one another. She expresses to Will her desire to make life beautiful for all and her sorrow at the thought of anyone's being deprived of a decent life. Will calls this a "fanaticism of sympathy." He thinks one should enjoy life whenever one can, and by this enjoyment one contributes happiness to the world. He also suggests that Dorothea is seeking martyrdom or self-punishment. Dorothea feels Will misunderstands, and argues that she is just idealistic and emotional. Will, who becomes very emotional, exclaims that Dorothea gives the impression of never having had any childhood and of suffering a great deal. He warns her that now she is going to Lowick to suffocate morally and aesthetically in the stifling, oppressive atmosphere of Casaubon's prison. Dorothea, in determined tone, asserts, "Lowick is my chosen home."

> **COMMENT:** Ladislaw is unable to appreciate the idealism of Dorothea. Recall how Eliot stresses the obstacles which the realities of life place before idealists.

Dorothea, remembering what Will had said the other day about Casaubon's neglect of German scholarship, questions him as to the possibility of her husband's chances of succeeding without German information. Will answers slightingly. "How can you bear to speak so lightly?" Dorothea angrily asks. She also is beginning to understand the hopelessness of her husband's project, yet she defends him on the theory that "to fail grandly" is better than never to have made an attempt. Will, now concurring with this view, reveals his plan to forsake Casaubon's generosity by returning to England to become independent. He believes that Dorothea does not really love Casaubon, but her pride and stubbornness motivate her to serve him. He is ready to leave, apologizing to her for hurting her (by suggesting ideas for Casaubon's failure), but she expresses a fondness for him and wishes him success in his new venture. He offers his help to her if she ever needs it.

Later, Dorothea tells Casaubon of Will's new determination but he is interested only listlessly. At his request, Dorothea will not mention Will's name again. It is interesting to note that Casaubon uses terms of endearment only when his manner is "the coldest."

COMMENT: Dorothea is unwilling to betray her loyalty to Casaubon in the face of his probable failure as a scholar. Will Ladislaw's decision to return to England is not un-mixed with an egotistical evaluation of his own abilities, not unlike the foolish pride which has blinded Casaubon to the truth about his scholarly failures.

BOOK THREE—WAITING FOR DEATH

CHAPTER TWENTY-THREE

Fred Vincy is in trouble. He is in debt to Mr. Bambridge, a horse dealer who had lent him one hundred sixty pounds, which he has squandered. Bambridge required security, so Fred had obtained a note with Caleb Garth's signature. As we know, Fred had felt sure of receiving a present from his uncle; he had also put faith in his ability to sell a horse for profit; if all failed, he had hoped to solicit money from his father. The Vincys all lived prodigally, but the thought of his mother's sorrow and his father's disagreeableness discouraged Fred's inclination to borrow there. To whom does one usually turn when in debt? Why, to a poor friend who is most likely to extend himself at a great risk. As Eliot states, "One must be poor to know the luxury of giving." So Fred turned to Caleb, who had a high opinion of Fred and was sure Fred would turn out well. The Vincys are socially prominent, so they feel "superior" to the Garths. There is a slight family connection between the families through Featherstone's two marriages (the first to Mr. Garth's sister, and the second to Mrs. Vincy's sister). Mr. Garth had a business failure, but has managed through hard work to pay his debts and redeem himself well. According to Middlemarch society, however, he was of the "lower" class, regardless of his spotless character. The children of the two families have always enjoyed a close relationship and Fred holds Mr. Garth in high opinion. He wishes to repay the note as quickly as possible to keep Mr. Garth's respect for him. Mr. Garth is absorbed in work on Sir James Chettam's farm buildings, and has neglected to tell his wife of the signature on the note.

Fred, moreover, has failed his exams and his father is livid with rage over debts he has incurred at school. Mr. Vincy, knowing Fred to be Featherstone's favorite heir, however, curbs his disfavor. Fred is aware of his father's thinking. The time for the payment of the debt is near, and Fred is still short of the sum. Of the hundred pounds he has received from his uncle, he deposits eighty with his mother and loses the other twenty at billiards. He next devises the plan of setting out to the horse fair with experienced horsemen (Horrock the veterinarian and Bambridge), to obtain their advice indirectly. He withdraws the eighty pounds from his mother's safekeeping, then buys a horse, Diamond, from a farmer for thirty pounds and his horse as a swap. He mistakenly believes that it is a good buy. He intends to sell it at a profit to Lord Medlicote, who is in the market for a horse. Fred is on his way home with high hopes of reducing his debt to almost nothing.

COMMENT: The scene between Fred Vincy, Bambridge, and the others at the Houndsley horse fair shows Eliot's great skill in capturing with realistic details the affairs of rural English life in the nineteenth century.

CHAPTER TWENTY-FOUR

Diamond, while in his stall, displays a violent nature; after almost killing the groom, he proceeds to lame himself by catching his leg in a rope. Now Fred has but fifty pounds and with the note due in five days, little prospect of increasing his capital. Normally, Fred would have procrastinated in hope of Providence's providing a way out, but his love for Mary and respect for Caleb urge him to face up to the situation. Nevertheless, Fred is despondent, thinking of the interviews ahead. Mr. Garth is not in his office, so Fred proceeds to the Garth home. The family is a happy one and Fred is quite at home there. There are four boys and two girls, including Mary. It is a simple home, with nothing rich except love and hospitality. Mrs. Garth is a sensible, patient, good-natured woman who accepts what is unalterable and understands, loves, and helps Caleb. She is fond of Fred in a motherly way, and often excuses his follies. She is busily teaching grammar and baking when Fred arrives. Mrs. Garth has saved ninety-two pounds for her son Alfred's education. When Fred hears this news, he is ashamed. Mr. Garth arrives; Fred tells him of the situation—much to the surprise of Mrs. Garth, who had been uninformed. With the Christmas holidays approaching, Mr. Garth is worried about his financial situation, but Mrs. Garth offers her ninety-two pounds and pledges money of Mary's for the rest. She realizes that Caleb is crushed and gently reprimands him; first, for not telling her about the note and, second, for being so charitable as to perform work often for nothing. However, with Mrs. Garth's ninety-two pounds and Mary's money they will meet the note.

Caleb had been fascinated by the land at an early age; apprenticed to a surveyor, he came to know more of management, building, and mining than most professionals. He considers it to be highly dignified work and he is most happy and at peace doing it; however, he cannot manage his own money, with the result that he runs his family into constant financial difficulty.

> **COMMENT:**   George Eliot's father was an estate manager, whose duties were like those of Caleb Garth. Witness the sympathetic treatment of Caleb's inability to manage his money, and the emphasis that the Garth family places on love and respect in preference to mere affluence.

CHAPTER TWENTY-FIVE

Fred wants to visit Mary before Caleb arrives to tell her that she will have to give him the part of her savings pledged by her mother. She is at Stone Court. Fred is remorseful. "I am a good-for-nothing blackguard scoundrel." Mary begins to cry when he tells her about the debt. He asks Mary to ask his uncle for a loan to send her brother Alfred to school, but Mary refuses flatly: the Garths do not beg. Fred pleads that he is merely unfortunate like other men often are, and uses Mr. Garth's bankruptcy as an example. Mary is incensed; she replies that her father lost his money by thinking of work to be done for others, not following his own idle pleasure. When Fred asks forgiveness, Mary candidly asks him if he thinks forgiveness will restore the lost money. Fred promises to reform and to become anything she wants him to be, if she will say she loves him. Mary becomes somewhat more tender with him, but not to the point of complete forgiveness.

After Fred leaves, Caleb arrives and informs Mary of the debt. She offers him twenty-four pounds although he needs only eighteen; he proceeds to warn Mary of Fred's well-intentioned but useless ways. Young people often get married with illusions and soon enough find that it is much harder than they imagined, explains Garth. Mary reassures him that she "will never engage herself to one who has no independence and who goes on loitering away his time on the chance that others will provide for him."

CHAPTER TWENTY-SIX

On his way home, Fred becomes ill. His mother calls for Dr. Wrench (a small, neat, bilious man, with a well-dressed wig), who tells him he has a "slight derangement." He distributes the usual ineffective drugs, and when Fred attempts to carry on his usual routine after a few days, he becomes worse. Dr. Wrench cannot be found. Rosamond sees Dr. Lydgate passing by, and implores her mother to call him. Lydgate tells them that Fred has typhoid fever in its early stages and puts him on complete bedrest. Mrs. Vincy is distraught, but vents her displeasure about Dr. Wrench's neglect. She wants Lydgate to continue attending Fred. Her husband is also angry with Wrench, yet is more annoyed at the "inconvenience" caused by Fred's fever. Lydgate is now the family doctor for the Vincy family. Dr. Wrench does not take his dismissal from the case kindly; he is inclined to place the blame upon Lydgate for the whole situation, since he is a younger man with less experience.

CHAPTER TWENTY-SEVEN

Fred is delirious and Mrs. Vincy pleads with Lydgate to "save him." Rosamond cooperates with the doctor to calm her mother. When Fred's crisis passes, Lydgate finds himself thinking more of Rosamond. According to her "theory" of love—that close proximity breeds love—this opportunity for prolonged contact should prove fruitful. After the quarantine is lifted, Lydgate decides that a little harmless flirtation with Rosamond will enliven their relationship. To Rosamond, however, flirtation is a sign of love. She feels he is far superior to her other admirers: he wears the right clothes, is knowledgeable on various subjects, and has the proper manners and accent of a university man. She sees only the façade of the man, and Lydgate sees only her beauty, cleverness, and amiability.

Lydgate, however, has made enemies in Middlemarch, although it has been unintentional on his part. One in particular is Mr.

Ned Plymdale, who is seeking Rosamond's affection but has been rebuffed. He becomes jealous of the time Rosamond spends with Lydgate; Rosamond thinks that she and Lydgate are practically "engaged." That evening Lydgate still seems to be more interested in his study of primitive tissue; he also senses an imminent feud with the other medical men, especially when Bulstrode's plans for managing the new hospital are announced.

CHAPTER TWENTY-EIGHT

Reverend and Mrs. Casaubon return home to Lowick Manor in the middle of January. It now seems to Dorothea that the house is smaller and more confining. The furniture seems to have shrunk; the books in the bookcase appear artificial.

> **COMMENT:** Eliot uses images in the room's physical setting to evoke a mood. Dorothea's gloomy response to her home suggests that her hopes for success and happiness in her marriage have also shrunk.

Only Dorothea and the house's fire are aglow with life. She is anxious for her wifely duties to begin, so she may share her husband's destiny. She asks, "What shall I do?" "Whatever you please, my dear," answers Casaubon.

Dorothea is becoming a moral prisoner, as Will Ladislaw had prophesied. She is disenchanted; her religious fervor is a "solitary cry in the night." Casaubon, who is not feeling well, retires to the library. Mr. Brooke and Celia unexpectedly visit the Casaubons. Mr. Brooke does not see the disillusionment in Dorothea and mentions to her that her husband appears pale, a fact which she has failed to notice. Dorothea sees that her sister is blushing, and Celia finally reveals that she and Sir James Chettham are to be married. Dorothea is pleased; she tells Celia that she believes Sir James to be a "good, honorable man."

CHAPTER TWENTY-NINE

The chapter begins with an analysis of Casaubon's thoughts concerning his marriage. With all his frigidity of manner and speech, and lack of joy in most things not concerning his study, he still has an "intense consciousness" and is "spiritually a-hungered like the rest of us." His criteria for judging a woman's suitability for marriage were age (the younger the better), submissiveness, a social rank equal to his, moral principles, virtue, and understanding. Aware of his age and afraid he would miss the advantages of being married, he began to seek a wife. In Dorothea he had seen the perfect choice, viewing her also as a good potential secretary, although never considering her rights to happiness in marriage. He was doubtful of the power of his mind, but knew Dorothea believed he was capable of great work and was flattered. Scrupulous, and not blessed with a strong body, Casaubon is a sensitive man but too languid to feel or express enthusiasm about anything. Afraid to show his feelings to Dorothea, he now holds great misgivings about his own power as a scholar. He cannot experience any of the joys of life, since his chief concern is the preservation of his reputation for scholarship.

While Dorothea and Casaubon are at work in the library, he pauses to offer her a two-page letter from Will Ladislaw, remarking that he hopes that she does not ask Will to visit them, because he has no leisure "to waste" on Will. Dorothea is shocked and angry that he prejudges her and underestimates her concern for his privacy. Leaving Will's letter unread, she retires; a short time later he hears the slam of a book on the floor of the library. Casaubon has suffered a heart attack! Celia and Sir James arrive to visit the Casaubons. They send for Dr. Lydgate, who arrives promptly to attend to the stricken man.

CHAPTER THIRTY

Casaubon begins to recover after a few days. Dr. Lydgate advises moderation and variety of relaxation. He has planned to speak to Dorothea about her husband's condition; he is motivated by psychological as well as medical reasons. Dorothea beseeches him to tell her the truth about Casaubon. He advises her that he could live for fifteen years or that he could die suddenly. Casaubon is not to be informed of these possibilities because of the anxiety it might cause him. He tells her that above all else he must avoid consternation. Dorothea feels guilty about the letters from Will and her behavior in the library prior to her husband's attack.

She later reads Will's letters. He tells of his appreciation for the help given him by Casaubon; he is anxious to do well on his own in order to show that Casaubon's good faith was not in vain. He announces his arrival in England and his intention to visit them in order to deliver the picture of Casaubon (called "The Dispute"), painted by Adolf Naumann. The other letter continues their discussion on art begun in Rome. Dorothea, afraid that this visit will cause excessive anxiety for her husband, asks her uncle to write to Will requesting him to postpone a visit to Lowick because of her husband's illness. As Mr. Brooke is writing the letter, he decides to invite Will to Tipton Grange. He has purchased the *Middlemarch Pioneer,* a newspaper he intends to use to further his political ambitions, and since Celia is leaving to marry, a young man with Will's potential will be pleasant to have working for him. Mr. Brooke, however, neglects to reveal this invitation to Dorothea.

CHAPTER THIRTY-ONE

Rosamond Vincy is elated when she thinks that Lydgate has now attended to two of the finest families of Middlemarch: Sir James Chettam's and Casaubon's. She feels it must be dreadful for Dorothea to have to live with a sick or dying man. Lydgate's frequent visits to Rosamond have given Middlemarch society something about which to gossip, and Mrs. Bulstrode, who was never really satisfied with her sister's marriage, is now determined to see Rosamond's future husband become socially prominent. We find her frequenting the house of Mrs. Plymdale for the purpose of arranging a match with Ned Plymdale and her niece. Mrs. Plymdale believes that there is "something" between Rosamond and Dr. Lydgate. Mrs. Bulstrode is shocked to hear of their rumored engagement. She goes to visit her niece.

Mrs. Bulstrode confronts Rosamond with the rumor but Rosamond denies it, saying she cares little about social gossip. Her aunt reminds her that she is now twenty-two and will receive no fortune from her father. She attempts to discourage Rosamond's interest in Lydgate, giving the following reasons: he is poor; his profession is not well thought of in Middlemarch; and he has no real principles. Rosamond displays a calm but determined will to do what she has resolved. Mrs. Bulstrode warns Rosamond about the possible loss of the high style of living she is accustomed to and offers Ned Plymdale, a man, she suggests, who will be able to offer her everything she needs for marriage. Rosamond refuses him and affects a "tortured heroine" reaction.

Mrs. Bulstrode considers it is her duty to arrange a meeting with Lydgate to ask him about his intentions. She then tells him that he should not take up so much of Rosamond's time unless he intends to marry her. When Mr. Farebrother makes a remark about the romantic notions of the girls of Middlemarch concerning Lydgate, the doctor decides to visit the Vincy household only when necessary. Rosamond is very unhappy when she misses him for two days. She begins to feel the pangs of unrequited love, but she is not disposed to any desperate act. She does not know Lydgate's reasons for neglecting her and is, therefore, very cold to him when he makes a visit. She involuntarily begins to cry; Lydgate suddenly thinks that he does love her and wishes to marry her. They seek out Mr. Vincy, who gives his consent at once.

> **COMMENT:** This last scene is conveyed by description and narrative comment. It achieves its effect by the way emotions are expressed chiefly by physical postures and gestures; only one line of dialogue is used. Lydgate asks Rosamond, "What is the matter? You are distressed. Tell me—pray." Her unusual naturalness has captured Lydgate; he becomes trapped into marriage and so ruins both their lives. Only here and one other time, later in the novel, does Rosamond stop living in her fantasy world sufficiently to transcend her egoism. Ironically, as we shall see, the second time she saves Dorothea and Ladislaw. But it is not love which binds Lydgate to Rosamond; it is affection, tenderness, and his consciousness of having hurt her.
>
> As Lydgate begins, so must he go on; he will be disillusioned; the beginning foreshadows the end. Unlike Casaubon, whose emotions are buried in a sealed tomb, we see that Lydgate's are in a sepulchre; it is not sealed; his are released at the slightest concussion.
>
> An appropriate image used repeatedly by Eliot in this

chapter is the "chain"—a symbol of entanglement, bonds, and fetters.

CHAPTER THIRTY-TWO

All of Peter Featherstone's greedy relatives become interested in his will when they realize that he is close to death. His brother Solomon and sister Jane are wealthy themselves, yet they are confident Peter will not overlook them; they think it natural that he should keep away his less-favored brother Jonah and sister Martha. The clan flocks to his house but Peter does not wish to see any of them. Mrs. Vincy is helping to advise the servants on how to handle the influx of relatives. Brother Jonah perches in the kitchen prepared to await his brother's death. (Notice the vulture image.) He watches Mary Garth with beady, suspicious eyes. She is much annoyed, and tells Fred of the spectacle; he howls with laughter, but attempts to relieve her distress through a verbal attack on the relatives. Brother Solomon and sister Jane Waule are there every day for hours. Dressed in black, they ignore Peter's orders and present themselves at the door, although he is enraged. They are very upset to see Mrs. Vincy and Fred, for fear that these two may have encouraged their brother to change his will in their favor. Featherstone's cousin Borthrop Trumbull (who is also his business advisor) takes a fancy to Mary Garth, expecting that Peter will find it in his heart to be kind to her in his will. Solomon declares he does not care to whom Peter leaves his money as long as they deserve it. (This comment is directed at Mary.) Trumbull is suspected of knowing the contents of the will; Jane and Solomon attempt to learn its contents from him. He tells them nothing (he really does not know the contents) and enjoys watching their reaction. He tells Solomon that Mary is a sensible girl and "minds" what she is doing. Solomon retorts that one can wager Peter "has left that girl a lumping sum."

CHAPTER THIRTY-THREE

That night, after midnight, while Mary is sitting up with Featherstone, she thinks of how ridiculous his relatives are in pretending to be interested in his welfare. Mary has particular disdain for Mrs. Vincy's attitude about Fred, and she wonders how Fred will react if he is excluded from Peter's will, which she suspects is going to happen. At three o'clock, Featherstone calls her to his side and asks her how many relatives are in the house. He then tells her that they are all fools. He asserts that he knows what their motives are. He reveals that he has had two wills drawn up, and now wishes to burn one of them. Mary does not wish to be open to suspicion by helping him to do such an act, so he demands that she call Fred Vincy. Mary does not want to have Fred implicated, so she agrees to burn one of the wills, only if he will call Jonah and the others. He refuses; Mary then urges him to call a lawyer. Peter orders her to open a chest, and to remove the money in it. It is hers if she will oblige him; he avows that no one knows it is there. Mary refuses again. In anger Peter throws a stick at her, but it falls to the floor. Since dawn is rapidly approaching, Mary puts more wood on the fading fire. But before morning arrives, Peter Featherstone is dead.

BOOK FOUR—THREE LOVE PROBLEMS

CHAPTER THIRTY-FOUR

Peter Featherstone is buried on a cloudy and chilly morning in May. Word has spread that it is to be a "big burying"; old Featherstone had left directions to make sure he had a funeral "beyond his betters." He had loved to spend money on his peculiar tastes, but best of all he had loved to make people feel uncomfortable through the power of his money. He had arranged the funeral with imagination and certainly enjoyed the anticipation, foregoing, of course, the proceedings. The three mourning coaches are met by the clergyman, Mr. Cadwallader. Fred chose him instead of Casaubon, who was of his own parish, because Fred did not want to suffer through his sermon. Mrs. Cadwallader watches (with Celia and Sir James) from an upper window in their house at Lowick. Celia remarks that she can endure no more, but observes that Dorothea enjoys it because she likes melancholy things. Mr. Brooke arrives and comments that Casaubon has returned and is in the library studying.

Discussing the various people attending the funeral, they notice a man with whom they are not familiar. All are struck by his odd appearance: ". . . bulging eyes, a sort of frog-face. . . ." Celia chides Dorothea about not telling her that Ladislaw had arrived. Mr. Brooke intervenes, explaining that Will is staying with him at the Grange, and that they have the picture of Casaubon painted in Rome by Adolf Naumann. Upon hearing the news, Casaubon remembers that he had not seen Will's letter when he became ill; he now concludes that Dorothea had asked her uncle to invite him to visit. When Dorothea realizes what her husband thinks has happened, she is disturbed but careful not to make a scene. In the meantime, Mr. Brooke has gone to meet Ladislaw.

CHAPTER THIRTY-FIVE

George Eliot compares the relatives at the reading of Peter Featherstone's will to the animals which gathered on Noah's Ark to "feed on the same store of fodder." The Featherstone blood has allied itself against the Vincys and Mary Garth. What disturbs them most of all is the strange-looking man seen at the funeral. Some have seen him before at Featherstone's but paid little attention to his presence. Now, in their greedy anxiety, they are even more concerned with the identity of the "frog-faced" man. Mr. Standish, the lawyer, expects to read the last of three wills he had drawn up for Mr. Featherstone. He is surprised to find only two wills. The first (and ineffectual) will, dated August 9, 1825, bequeathed ten thousand pounds to Fred Vincy; the land and properties were to be given to Joshua Rigg, the frog-faced man. He was to be the sole executor and was to take the name of Featherstone. The greedy relatives were to receive small sums. But there is a second (and valid) will dated March 1, 1826, and a codicil (additional) to this will.

This will was the one the dying Featherstone wanted Mary Garth to burn. Mr. Standish is told to read the second will. It revokes the bequests to all but Rigg, who is to receive "all the land lying in Lowick parish, with all the stock and household furniture." The remainder is to be used for the construction of Featherstone's Alms-Houses for old men.

> **COMMENT:**   Disappointed and indignant, all of Featherstone's relatives now reveal their true dislike for him. Fred feels ill from the reading of the will, for Featherstone's second will was probably written to punish Fred for borrowing money.

Mary tells Fred he is better off without the money. Fred childishly fears he cannot repay the money which Caleb and Mary used to pay his note; now he must go into the ministry. Mary will have to seek another job to support herself.

> **COMMENT:**   Another stranger, Joshua Rigg, has come to Middlemarch; although he is a "visible thorn," no one yet knows what his plans are.

CHAPTER THIRTY-SIX

Mr. Vincy's outlook changes now that Fred has been left nothing; he warns Fred that he had better pass his examinations.

Fred, who only twenty-four hours ago had expectations of paying his debts and becoming a gentleman of leisure, is crushed completely. He was sure Mary would have married him once he inherited the money.

Mr. Vincy refuses to give his consent for Rosamond to marry Lydgate, because he "hasn't a farthing." Mrs. Vincy is distressed because Rosamond has already begun preparations for the wedding; moreover, Mr. Bulstrode favors the match. Rosamond dismisses discussion of financial matters, particularly any mention of a dowry to Lydgate, yet she makes lavish preparations for their home. Mr. Vincy does not discuss matters with Lydgate, preferring to play the gratuitous host, whom no one criticizes. Lydgate continues to spend most of his evenings at their home. He and Rosamond continue to spin their "gossamer web." She finally reveals her father's objections to the marriage. Lydgate tells her that if she is unhappy at home they should hasten their marriage. They agree on a date six weeks hence and begin to make plans for their home and for the wedding journey. Mr. Vincy makes certain that Lydgate has insured his life. Rosamond wrangles a promise from Lydgate that he will bring her to Quallingham, the home of his titled uncle Godwin, for a visit. She also hopes that he will find employment elsewhere than in Middlemarch.

CHAPTER THIRTY-SEVEN

COMMENT: In the beginning of this chapter, George Eliot discusses the political situation of the era. George IV is dead. The cry for reform is upon the land—Tory leaders themselves are in favor of liberal measures, such as the Catholic Emancipation Act and the Reform Bill. Such Tory stalwarts as the Duke of Wellington and Lord Grey are enthusiastically pushing for reform; only the House of Lords threatens to block these measures. At this point Lord Grey persuades King William IV (1830–1837), to threaten the creation by royal prerogative of enough new Whig peers to put the Reform Bill through the House of Lords. It is finally passed on June 4, 1832.

Will is anxious to work on the Middlemarch newspaper; he goes to see Dorothea not only to ask advice, but to visit her as well. Casaubon has gone to see the archdeacon; Dorothea is alone. Will tells her of the offer and she later tells her husband of Will's visit. He shows much displeasure. Later that evening, he writes a letter to Will expressing his objections to Will's taking a job with Mr. Brooke.

Because Dorothea spends so much time alone, she has the opportunity to think of the family's poor treatment of Will's grandmother. She was cut off from the family inheritance and from family protection because her family did not approve of the man she married. Dorothea thinks this situation should be righted, and she mentions it to her husband, suggesting that he make provision in his will to give his cousin Will half of his estate. Casaubon becomes enraged; he forbids Dorothea to mention the matter again.

The following day, Casaubon receives a reply from Will; it tells him that he intends to take the job with Mr. Brooke, regardless of the objections of his benefactor. Casaubon is filled with disgust and suspicion, but can turn to no one for advice because he is distrustful of everyone's feelings toward him. He remains silent.

CHAPTER THIRTY-EIGHT

Sir James Chettam is dissatisfied with Mr. Brooke's interest in politics. He goes to visit the Cadwalladers because discussion of this upsets Celia. They believe Mr. Brooke's campaign will result in failure. Rumors are that Ladislaw is "a quill-driving alien, a foreign emissary, and what not." In discussing the good and bad points of Mr. Brooke's decision, Mr. Cadwallader thinks that a loss may make him more conscious of the management of his estate. Sir James reflects that the management of his estate would improve only if he were to rehire Caleb Garth, whom he had fired twelve years earlier.

Mr. Brooke enters, and the group discusses with him the highly critical article written about him in the town's rival newspaper, *The Trumpet*. The article suggests that "a certain landlord" (Brooke) advocates reform methods for other farms, but does little regarding his own farm, except to collect the rents. Brooke believes that the people of Middlemarch are backward and need to be educated. They all agree that if a man decides to enter public life, he must be willing to accept the attendant consequences, which often take the form of ridicule and involve expense.

>   **COMMENT:** Mr. Brooke, like Dorothea and Dr. Lydgate, will discover that one's ideas and ambitions, however worthy in themselves, are always subject to the harsh realities of everyday existence.

CHAPTER THIRTY-NINE

Sir James thinks Dorothea could dissuade her uncle from entering politics and instead concentrate on making reforms in the management of his estate. He arranges for her to meet Brooke at the Grange. Mr. Brooke tells her that he hopes she is not getting too "learned" for a woman. Dorothea "pours forth" her emotions, telling him of how he might make vast improvements in his estate. He is stunned to realize how much help she could be, but decides to ignore her advice.

Will Ladislaw takes this opportunity to tell Dorothea of his correspondence with Reverend Casaubon, who forbade him to visit his home again. Dorothea feels wretched; she thinks her husband is completely wrong.

After his visit with Dorothea, Mr. Brooke finds it necessary to make an infrequent visit to one of his tenants, a man named Dagley. The man speaks loudly and disrespectfully to Mr. Brooke, who is astonished to find that he is not as popular a landlord as he had believed.

>   **COMMENT:** The tenant Dagley has a dog who is as disagreeable as his master. Eliot uses both to symbolize the bitter anger of English farmers caused by the agricultural depression and the resulting penury of the farms.

CHAPTER FORTY

This chapter returns us to Caleb Garth and his family. Mary Garth must look for a new position after the death of Peter

Featherstone. She has decided to go to York to teach, although
she is not fond of schoolrooms. While they are eating breakfast,
Caleb opens a letter he has received from Sir James, requesting
that he manage Brooke's estates. It will be a position with more
than adequate pay; Mary will not have to leave. His wife considers the offer a blessing.

The vicar of St. Botolph's, Mr. Farebrother, pays a visit to the
family that evening. He wishes to see not only Caleb and his
wife, but Mary also. He tells them that he has come as an envoy
of Fred Vincy, who has been out of town at school for many
months. The vicar remarks that Fred is trying again for his
degree, although he does not wish to enter the ministry. The
couple.agrees that he should not enter the church.

CHAPTER FORTY-ONE

The transactions between Mr. Bulstrode and Mr. Joshua Rigg
Featherstone for the sale of certain property at Stone Court begin. (Notice the name added to "Rigg," a condition required in
Peter Featherstone's will.) Joshua is, as always, "sleek, neat,
and cool as the frog he resembled." He had been brought up in
a seaport town and had been educated in small commercial
houses at the seaport. He has little respect for the rural Featherstones.

We are introduced to a new character, John Raffles, Joshua's
stepfather. He is nearly sixty, stout of figure, and swaggering of
air; his hair is thick, curly, and graying. The avaricious Raffles
is interested in his stepson's wealth, but Joshua remembers Raffles' cruel treatment and neglect of him as a child. He therefore
refuses to do more than provide a small weekly dole to Raffles'
wife as long as Raffles is alive. He fears that Raffles will seize
any large sum he might give her. Instead of showing defeat,
Raffles good-naturedly asks for a drink and his carfare to return. He then observes, "There's nothing I like better than
plaguing you." Raffles puts his brandy flask in his pocket. He
picks up a piece of paper which has fallen to the ground and
shoves it under the flask (which fits loosely in his pocket), in
order to hold it firm.

COMMENT: Unknown to Raffles, the piece of paper he has picked up to use to steady his brandy flask is a letter from Mr. Bulstrode. This letter contains significant information about Bulstrode's past; as we shall see, Raffles will want money to remain silent about the information contained in this letter.

CHAPTER FORTY-TWO

Dr. Lydgate, upon returning from his honeymoon, is requested to schedule his visits so as to include Reverend Casaubon. The Reverend, instead of assembling his notes and writing the "Key to All Mythologies," has something else on his mind which makes him inquisitive about his real state of health. Will Ladislaw haunts him; Dorothea seems to "judge" him. Although she is a model wife, Casaubon is suspicious of her ardent nature; when she is silent he mistakes it for a suppressed rebellion. Hadn't she asked her uncle to invite Will? Hadn't she requested that he should give Ladislaw half of his estate?

Casaubon requests Dr. Lydgate to reveal to him the whole truth about his illness. He wants to know its nature and his chances for the future. Finally, Lydgate admits that death can be sudden in illnesses such as his. After the doctor's departure, Casaubon rebuffs Dorothea. He secretly envisions her marrying Will after his death. He becomes reconciled with her, however, after spending time alone in the library. He treats her kindly and says, "Come my dear, come. You are young and need not extend your life by watching."

COMMENT: This utterance is the closest to real feeling that Casaubon will ever make to Dorothea.

BOOK FIVE—THE DEAD HAND

CHAPTER FORTY-THREE

Dorothea is anxious to learn everything about her husband's illness and the concern it is causing him, lest she offend him unknowingly. She visits Dr. Lydgate but he is not at home. Rosamond is there, for Dorothea hears her playing music; a man's voice can also be heard. When they meet, both women are anxious to appraise one another. As they are talking, much to the delightful surprise of Dorothea, Will Ladislaw steps forth and offers to fetch Dr. Lydgate, who is busy at the new hospital. Realizing how displeased Casaubon would be with this scene, Dorothea declines Will's offer and decides to seek the doctor herself. She reflects on the preceding events, thinking it improper that Will should remain with Rosamond in her husband's absence. She begins to sob: her image of Will is slightly spoiled. He, also, is humiliated because he senses that Dorothea does not approve of his presence with Rosamond.

Will tells Rosamond how he worships Dorothea and thinks of her as a "perfect woman." Later, Rosamond tells her husband about Dorothea's visit and Will's remarks to her about Dorothea. Lydgate remarks that Ladislaw is a "poor devil" for adoring Dorothea.

> **COMMENT:** With his comment about Ladislaw, Lydgate reveals his own weakness in marriage. He lacks the strength needed to speak out against his wife's expenditures, although he realizes that he cannot now devote his full energies to his work.

CHAPTER FORTY-FOUR

Dorothea visits Dr. Lydgate at the New Hospital and learns that there is no change in her husband's condition. The doctor takes this opportunity to question Dorothea about her awareness of the hospital's needs. She is very interested because, for the first time since her marriage, she sees an opportunity to be "useful." Dr. Lydgate explains that through Mr. Bulstrode's efforts and money, projects are making great strides, but some of the medical men and a few others are causing a disturbance. Lydgate feels their opposition is due partly to their dislike of Bulstrode and partly to their jealousy.

> **COMMENT:** The immediate motive for the opposition is that Bulstrode has placed the medical directorship in Lydgate's hands.

Dr. Lydgate explains that regardless of opposition and personal inconvenience, he will continue fighting for the benefit of science and the medical profession. Bulstrode can be of great help to Lydgate's projects, and so he sees no harm in cooperating with Bulstrode to achieve these ends. Dorothea is grateful to Dr. Lydgate for his information and praises him for his high ideals. She wishes she could "awake every morning" with the satisfying knowledge of her value and service to the world. Later, she asks her husband if she may donate two hundred pounds a year to the New Hospital. Casaubon agrees. Without questioning her about her interview with Lydgate, he remains distrustful of her affections.

CHAPTER FORTY-FIVE

> **COMMENT:** The bulk of this chapter shows us (as the reactions of people to Dr. Lydgate are reported), a cross-section of nineteenth-century English characters, particularly those in the medical profession.

Lydgate and Bulstrode view the opposition to the New Hospital in different lights. Lydgate considers it a mixture of jealousy and prejudice; Bulstrode sees it as a personal vendetta prompted by the distrust of the people and their hatred of his ministerial views and affiliation. Most of the gossip is repititious but it is heard from all social levels: from the conservative Dr. Minchen to the superstitious Mrs. Dollop, the landlady of the Tankard in Slaughter Land. (The latter is convinced that Dr. Lydgate wishes to kill patients for purposes of experimentation and research!) But Lydgate quickly develops lines of friendship and loyalty to overcome the early distrust and opposition.

COMMENT: Dr. Lydgate has incurred the dislike of several Middlemarch doctors because:

1. He sees little value in the dispensing of various medicines. His patients therefore correctly assume that they have long been paying money for worthless drugs.

2. He has effected certain cures which Middlemarchers consider miraculous; such cures reflect unfavorably on other doctors who earlier misdiagnosed the illnesses.

Bulstrode is anxious to solicit as much money as possible for maintaining the hospital, because he has designs on land tracts, and realizes that substantial capital will be needed to purchase them. His plan for management of the hospital is:

1. The hospital is to be reserved for fevers of all kinds.

2. Lydgate is to be chief medical superintendent.

3. Lydgate is to hold the power of ultimate decision, which is to be irrevocable.

4. General management is to be in the hands of five directors associated with Bulstrode.

5. Members are to be replaced by the board itself.

6. Votes are to be allotted in proportion to the amount of contributions given.

All the medical men refuse to visit the new hospital, but Lydgate plans to bring in new doctors; Bulstrode backs his plan to organize a board of members who are in sympathy with them and who will go along with their demands. In a conversation with Reverend Farebrother, Lydgate is warned that he should not become obligated to Bulstrode; he should disassociate himself as much as possible. Farebrother also cautions him not to go too deeply into debt.

CHAPTER FORTY-SIX

New political activity in Middlemarch is apparent with the increased interest in the Reform Bill then being debated in

Parliament. Mr. Brooke hopes that the election of a new party will help his chances of winning a seat in Parliament. He and Will Ladislaw discuss what they believe are the most important aspects of reform; and Will becomes a noticeable figure in the town through his editorials and his speeches. No one in town knows that he is Casaubon's nephew. Lydgate disagrees with Will on Mr. Brooke's qualifications and on the Reform Bill. Many heated arguments ensue between Lydgate and Ladislaw. Rosamond and Lydgate are expecting a baby. Although he seems to have an avid interest in politics, Lydgate is actually more concerned with his own finances and his inability to pay a furniture bill. Wishing to save Rosamond from worry, however, he remains silent about his money problems.

CHAPTER FORTY-SEVEN

Ladislaw, sitting alone in his room, reflects about his life since he has returned to Middlemarch, for he is now unsure whether he has been wise in associating himself with Middlemarch, Mr. Brooke, and *The Pioneer*. Although he is devoted to Dorothea, he is somehow pleased that she is "unattainable." (He does not wish for Casaubon's death, as Casaubon suspects.) Ladislaw seems to enjoy the situation as it now is: he idealizes Dorothea but subconsciously is afraid that in reality she will disappoint his image should their relationship become any more personal.

The next morning Will decides to go to Lowick to church, just to see Dorothea. He knows he will be breaking Casaubon's commandment that he never visit again and seems to delight in the prospect of displeasing his uncle. At church, Will sees Dorothea, but he begins to feel uncomfortable when Casaubon enters, and soon: "utterly ridiculous, out of temper, and miserable." Dorothea appears as if she were repressing tears, probably from embarrassment. She and Casaubon leave the church without glancing back.

> **COMMENT:** Eliot draws a sharp contrast in this chapter between the way one pictures an event in one's imagination and the disappointing way the event occurs in reality.

CHAPTER FORTY-EIGHT

Distressed over the disagreement between her husband and Will, Dorothea senses that Will's appearance at church has eliminated any hope for a reconciliation between them, which she has secretly hoped for. Although Casaubon has some difficulty breathing and is annoyed about the incident, he continues to work diligently on his notebooks. Dorothea, because she lacks the comfort and love of a genuine human relationship, longs for companionship. She had found it to some degree in Will Ladislaw, but now he is gone and she is left with Casaubon's indifference and his stale scholarship. Before they retire, Casaubon solicits Dorothea's help in the library. He awakes in the middle of the night, complaining of difficulty in lying down. Dorothea reads to him, and he tells her feverishly to "mark" this or that. He seems to cover his material quicker than usual. Before going to sleep he tries to elicit a promise from her to carry out his "wishes" in the event of his death. She does not give him an answer because she believes that he might expect her to read through the vast amount of notes he has been taking. She understands now that he has clung to her knowing that only through her can he ever hope to publish his work. Yet she would devote herself to him and his work if he lived for another fifteen years—so why shouldn't she now promise to serve him in that capacity after his death? Dorothea hesitates. Perhaps, she fears, he wants something more, since he will not tell her what his wish is.

The night passes. Dorothea finally relents to herself and promises to give her husband an answer. When she goes to tell him, she finds him sitting with his head resting on his arms on a stone table. She speaks to him. But Dorothea never gives her answer. Casaubon is dead.

CHAPTER FORTY-NINE

Mr. Brooke and Sir James Chettam discuss Casaubon's will in the library at Lowick Grange. In a codicil (addition) to the will, in a rage of jealousy, Casaubon had stated that Dorothea was to forfeit the money left to her in the will if she ever married Will Ladislaw. Both men are shocked by this revelation and decide to protect Dorothea by keeping the contents of the will from her and by "protecting" her from Ladislaw.

> **COMMENT:** Mr. Brooke is responsible for the second suggestion because he cannot afford to lose Will now that he has proven himself an able assistant to him in his campaign for Parliament.

CHAPTER FIFTY

Dorothea is visiting her sister Celia and her new baby at Freshitt Hall. She is considering what action to take as the new owner of Lowick Manor, and tells her uncle that she wishes to return to the Manor to go through her husband's papers to discover what plans he may have made regarding the house. He urges her to wait, but she is impatient. Inadvertently, Celia tells her sister of the secret codicil. Dorothea is shocked, because she had never considered Will in the light that Casaubon had presented him, and now suddenly recognizes a strange longing towards Will. She returns to Lowick Manor to seek any personal message Casaubon may have left for her, but after a thorough search of his papers, she finds nothing.

Lydgate speaks to Dorothea of Mr. Farebrother as a possible candidate for the position vacated by her husband. (Lydgate wants to purge his conscience for the vote he had cast against Farebrother.) Dorothea questions his habit of gambling, but Lydgate thinks that Farebrother, given a little security, would give it up entirely. When Lydgate leaves, Dorothea abandons herself to thoughts of Will Ladislaw.

CHAPTER FIFTY-ONE

Parliament has been dissolved and election fever is high. Will has not seen Dorothea since the death of her husband. He has been working long hours at the newspaper for the forthcoming election. Mr. Brooke is running on the independent ticket and is jubilant; not even heavy expenses can daunt his enthusiasm. Ladislaw continues to pound the best arguments for Reform into the tangled mind of Mr. Brooke. Before the day of nomination, Brooke must explain his views to the electors. He is confident, for his reforms as a landlord have silenced the blasts of the *Trumpet,* and he hears himself cheered a little as he drives into town. He and his friends stop at the Green Dragon and Brooke, normally a nondrinker, has two glasses of sherry. He begins his speech well but the effect of the sherry causes him to muddle his train of thought. As he speaks, someone in the throng raises an effigy of his exact likeness. A parrotlike voice begins echoing his words and the crowd begins to laugh and to throw eggs. It is obvious that the candidacy of Brooke is an inglorious failure.

> **COMMENT:**   A political maneuver by Brooke's enemies combined with his own foolish drinking have brought about his defeat. Eliot suggests that the police may have been bribed to ignore the planned disruption of Brooke's speech. This chapter is valuable for its insights into provincial English politics.

Will is dejected and resolves to give up *The Pioneer* and Mr. Brooke. He plans to work earnestly at political writing and speaking, for which he has a talent. When he is established, he will come back to see Dorothea. She must not know his reason for not wishing to marry her now.

Mr. Brooke, in a roundabout manner, makes it evident that he, among others, wishes Will to "quit" *The Pioneer* and to leave Middlemarch. "I shall go of my own movement," thinks Will Ladislaw.

CHAPTER FIFTY-TWO

Dorothea asks Reverend Farebrother and his family to be the tenants at Lowick Manor. They are delighted. His sister suggests to the clergyman that now he is in a position to marry and Mary Garth would be a good choice. He advises her that a wife is not to be chosen "as poultry in a market." He does, however, promise them that he will forego his card playing.

A week later, Fred Vincy, who has received his degree from Omnibus College, comes to visit Farebrother. He tells him that he does not want to enter the church, but he does not know what else he might be able to do. He also confesses his love for Mary Garth to the vicar. He then asks him to speak to her for him! Although Farebrother is in love with Mary himself, he goes to her with Fred's request.

When he sees Mary, he praises Fred's sincerity and good nature; wisdom, he says, lies in these two qualities. He also tells her not to feel guilt for not burning Peter Featherstone's second will because, according to law, if the second were destroyed, the first would be of no consequence. He also tells Mary that Fred has received his degree and will comply with the wishes of his father, if she will forgive his previous actions and state her feelings about him. Unhesitatingly, Mary says she will not marry him if he becomes a clergyman, because she feels that Fred is totally unfitted for such a vocation; she has no respect for men who use the cloth to better their social position. She will marry Fred only when he proves himself to be a responsible person. Mary detects an emotional tremor in the vicar's voice, but dismisses a romantic thought as foolish folly. Farebrother leaves, reflecting that he has never performed a more difficult duty.

> **COMMENT:**   Eliot employs dramatic irony effectively in this chapter. The reader is aware that Farebrother is genuinely interested in marrying Mary Garth, yet he is placed in a position of speaking to her of another's love for her. Every word of Mary's about Fred has special meaning for Farebrother, which only he and the reader can perceive.

CHAPTER FIFTY-THREE

Joshua Rigg surprises everyone by selling Stone Court to Mr. Bulstrode, thereby giving him even greater power in Middlemarch. Joshua's real ambition is to become a moneychanger. Peter Featherstone's relatives are delighted to hear the news, because they consider the dead man's wishes as expressed in his will to have been ignored.

Bulstrode is discussing stable drainage with Caleb Garth when a man in black rides forward to join them. The stranger is John Raffles, an acquaintance whom Bulstrode has not seen for twenty-five years. Garth leaves. Bulstrode suddenly turns pale, because he knows Raffles is familiar with events in his past life.

> **COMMENT:**   At this point, Eliot summarizes past in-
> cidents to show the significance Raffles' appearance
> has for Bulstrode. Years earlier, Bulstrode had married
> an elderly, wealthy widow, whose daughter, Sarah, had
> run away from home with her small baby. A search had
> been made for them and Raffles, discovering their where-
> abouts, had been paid by Bulstrode to remain silent. He
> sent Raffles to America and had inherited his wife's money
> when she died.

Bulstrode gives Raffles two hundred pounds "blackmail" hoping he will leave Middlemarch. Bulstrode's present wife and Middlemarch society know nothing of his earlier disreputable actions. Raffles remembers the name of Bulstrode's stepdaugh-ter. It is "Ladislaw"; Will Ladislaw is her son! Bulstrode fears that he will see John Raffles again.

BOOK SIX—THE WIDOW AND THE WIFE

CHAPTER FIFTY-FOUR

After Dorothea has been at Freshitt for three months, she becomes increasingly restless; over the objections of Celia, Sir James, and Mrs. Cadwallader, she makes plans to return to Lowick. Upon her return, she realizes that her real reason for returning to Lowick Manor is to see Will Ladislaw.

One morning, Will makes a call on her. They both appear uncomfortable but determined in their conversation. He tells her that he has come to say goodbye because he is leaving to start a new life in London. She thinks that he must know of the codicil to the will, then tells him that she will never forget him. Before they are able to say anything else about their true feelings, Sir James enters. Will leaves immediately, after bidding Dorothea goodbye.

CHAPTER FIFTY-FIVE

Dorothea is unaware that she has experienced the emotion called love. She feels she will never see Ladislaw again, and makes some firm resolutions for the future.

> **COMMENT:** Dorothea resolves that she will never remarry and will devote her time, money, and energy to the pursuit of happiness for others less fortunate than herself.

On a visit to Freshitt, Sir James, Celia, and Mrs. Cadwallader entreat Dorothea to remove her mourning cap. When she does, they exclaim about her beauty. Mrs. Cadwallader again approaches Dorothea on the subject of marriage and Dorothea reminds her that she is interested only in the idea of organizing a utopian society; she has consulted Mr. Garth about her plans. Sir James cannot think of Dorothea's remarrying either. He considers such an idea degrading and privately wishes her to choose solitude.

COMMENT: Dorothea is learning to substitute ideals for the love and happiness which a marriage to Will Ladislaw could have brought her.

CHAPTER FIFTY-SIX

Dorothea's interest in the building of cottages is renewed, especially because of her confidence in Caleb Garth and his approval of her ideas. She finds him to be the man best suited to manage her land at Lowick Manor.

Railroads are now being built through the smaller towns and villages. They are looked upon by many as being dangerous. The discussion of them is "as exciting a topic as the Reform Bill or the imminent horrors of cholera." One day, Peter Featherstone's brother, Solomon, is responsible for an uprising of tenant farmers against the railroad employees. Caleb Garth is having difficulty calming the angry farmers; just then, Fred Vincy offers to assist him. By coincidence, they both see in this effort a chance to improve their relationship; for Fred in particular, it is a way to prove himself to Mary.

Fred and Caleb, however, are the only members of both families pleased with Fred. Mrs. Garth fears that he may never become trustworthy. Mr. Vincy still thinks that Fred should enter the church.

CHAPTER FIFTY-SEVEN

That evening, Fred visits Lowick parsonage to call on Mrs. Garth. He assures her that he can be trusted to do a good job as Caleb's assistant. Even with Fred's reassurance, Mrs. Garth insists that Reverend Farebrother would be a better husband for Mary. Fred fails to realize that Mrs. Garth still looks unfavorably on him; he hopes, after he proves himself, that he will finally win Mary. Mary has secretly decided to marry Fred and to refuse Reverend Farebrother, who has declared his own interest to her.

CHAPTER FIFTY-EIGHT

Captain Lydgate, a cousin of the doctor, pays a visit to the home of Lydgate and Rosamond. He persuades her, against her husband's wishes, to go horseback riding; as a result, her baby is born prematurely and dies.

Having incurred numerous bills until he owes a total debt of three hundred and eighty pounds, Lydgate begins to worry more about his financial situation. Rosamond finally realizes that they are under increasing strain but refuses to halt her prodigal spending. When she suggests that Lydgate ask her father for money, he becomes enraged, although he forgives her almost immediately. Lydgate looks sadly forward, "with dread to the inevitable future discussion about expenditures and the necessity for a complete change in their way of living."

CHAPTER FIFTY-NINE

Because gossip in a small town spreads rapidly, it is not long before Rosamond hears of the codicil to Casaubon's will forbidding any marriage between Dorothea and Will. Although warned by Lydgate not to mention it to Will, she reveals it to him. He had not known of it until this time. He calls it a "foul insult" both to Dorothea and to himself; in anger, he tells Rosamond he will never marry Dorothea. Rosamond is concerned both with Will's anger toward her and with Lydgate's debts.

CHAPTER SIXTY

At the end of August, Mr. Bulstrode requests Will to judge the value of a painting he wishes to buy at an auction. Will agrees, using this request as an excuse for delaying his departure to London. During the bidding, a red-faced man with whiskers steps in front of Will and asks if his mother's name was Sarah Dunkirk. The stranger, who is Mr. Raffles, appears to have accurate knowledge of Will's family, although Will has never seen him before. Raffles tells Will that he once knew his father and mother. He also reveals to Will that his mother ran away from home when she was a "young lass." Will stumbles away from Raffles in his confusion over the information he has been given about his mother. He is certain, however that there could be nothing dishonorable about her behavior.

COMMENT: A colorful picture of an English country auction is presented in this chapter. It is also a key episode in the plot, because of Will's conversation with Raffles.

CHAPTER SIXTY-ONE

Raffles comes to Mr. Bulstrode's house; when he finds that he is not at home, he leaves abruptly. Realizing that the revelation of his past life will make him the object of scorn in Middlemarch, Bulstrode feels powerless to help himself. In a flashback, he sees himself as a young banker's clerk. He had become close friends with Mr. Dunkirk, the richest man in the congregation of the church. Eventually he became a confidential accountant in Mr. Dunkirk's pawnbroking business. He soon discovered that the business was receiving stolen goods, but he neither made an effort to leave, nor to do anything about it. He rationalized his part in the operation by saying that it was part of a divine plan. Years later, both Mr. Dunkirk and his only son died, leaving Mrs. Dunkirk alone, except for a daughter Sarah who ran away from home to go on the stage. Her decision was made when she realized the nature of her father's "business." Sarah had never been found. Bulstrode and the widow planned to marry but she refused until she had made a final search for her daughter. Sarah was found by Raffles, but the information was never revealed to Mrs. Dunkirk. The only persons who shared the secret were Bulstrode and Raffles, who was paid for keeping silent and remaining out of sight. Bulstrode married the widow Dunkirk, and subsequently became heir to all of her wealth when she died five years later.

COMMENT: Mrs. Dunkirk's lost daghter, Sarah, was the mother of Will Ladislaw. He, therefore, is the proper heir to the Dunkirk fortune.

Bulstrode goes to visit Will and reveals their connection. In order to prevent a scandal, he offers Will five hundred pounds a year and a share in his own estate after his death. Will speaks scornfully to Bulstrode. He tells him he wants no part of any money that was made dishonestly.

CHAPTER SIXTY-TWO

After leaving Bulstrode, Will plans to pay a final visit to Dorothea and then to leave Middlemarch. He writes a note to her,
but she is not at home when it arrives. Sir James, because of
his hatred for Will, has been spreading rumors of the friendship
between Will and Rosamond Lydgate. Dorothea defends Will
against the gossip but when she accidently meets him at Tipton
Grange and discovers that he is leaving for good, she wonders
if *he* fears possible involvement with Rosamond. Dorothea fails
to realize that it is because of her alone that he has made his
choice. Will's final words, however, reassure her that he loves
her truly. He leaves Middlemarch the following evening.

BOOK SEVEN—TWO TEMPTATIONS

CHAPTER SIXTY-THREE

Some of the townspeople, especially Reverend Farebrother, are aware that Lydgate is in financial difficulty. Lydgate prefers to keep his problems to himself, confiding in no one and asking assistance from no one (although Farebrother would be able to help him if he asked). It occurs to no one except Farebrother that Lydgate's marriage to Rosamond is not happy: she is becoming less attentive to her husband and to the problems she is creating for him.

> **COMMENT:** The disparity between the illusion Lydgate creates for others and the disappointing reality of his marriage to Rosamond is the major focus of this chapter.

CHAPTER SIXTY-FOUR

Finally, Lydgate realizes that he must make a last plea to Rosamond to be more economical in her way of life. Spoiled and childish, she begins to cry and refuses to change anything. In fact, she even accuses him of stinginess. Her only suggestions are that they leave Middlemarch so that he can find a better paying position; they can also seek the help of his uncle, Sir Godwin. Lydgate tells her that he has planned to rent their house so that they will have more money. Stubbornly refusing to do as he wishes, she writes to Lydgate's uncle for help and also writes to the renting agent, advising that they have changed their plans about renting the house. She tells Lydgate of neither of these letters.

Lydgate's eventual discovery of what she has done fills him with anger and despair; yet he realizes that she will not change her habits—eventually he must ask his uncle, Sir Godwin, for help.

CHAPTER SIXTY-FIVE

One morning, a letter comes in the mail addressed to Dr. Tertius

Lydgate. Rosamond notices that it is from Sir Godwin. Lydgate opens it and reads that his uncle is "not likely to have cash to spare." Lydgate accuses Rosamond of meddling; she accuses him of mistreating her, saying that it is she who has been wronged. Because he is kind-hearted and loves her, Lydgate again forgives her and even apologizes for his behavior. He tells her he realizes their situation is "ten times harder for her."

CHAPTER SIXTY-SIX

Lydgate, because of his anxiety about his present financial state, is unable to sustain any research or serious thought. At one time, he had resorted to the use of opium for temporary relief of mental strain; he had also tried alcohol and gambling, but they had never become a habit with him. He now feels that he must think of some means to raise some money to pay his debts. He believes that gambling is one way to win money quickly.

Lydgate meets Bambridge at the Green Dragon to discuss a horse that the latter was selling for him. While waiting for Bambridge, Lydgate plays a game of billiards; he begins to win and is covered by many bets. Fred Vincy and a friend, Hawley, arrive. Fred has been coming to the Green Dragon for several months to play and to converse with "men of pleasure" who frequent the tavern. He keeps a few pounds from his pay to wager if necessary. The last person he had expected to see was his stuffy brother-in-law, Dr. Lydgate, who is now playing as if his life depended on the outcome of the game. Young Hawley is beginning to get the best of Lydgate. Fred is in a dilemma as to what he should do to get Lydgate away from the game. He finally tells him that Reverend Farebrother is waiting to see him. This is enough to make Lydgate leave.

Later, Reverend Farebrother speaks to Fred, warning him that he will lose any chance of winning Mary if he should resort to his old ways of gambling. Fred realizes what a brave effort it was on the part of Farebrother to speak to Mary for him since he also loves her; at that moment he vows never to enter the Green Dragon again and to work harder to prove himself.

CHAPTER SIXTY-SEVEN

Since Sir Godwin has refused to assist Lydgate in his difficulties, the doctor unwillingly comes to the conclusion that there is no one for him to turn to but Mr. Bulstrode. He hesitates because of his dislike for Bulstrode. He receives a note from the banker: he wants to consult Lydgate at the bank about his "complaints." (Bulstrode has a tendency towards "hypochondria," or imaginary illnesses.)

Lydgate plans to use this opportunity to ask for a loan. Bulstrode is unsympathetic, because he has his own problems now with John Raffles. He coldly advises Lydgate to declare himself bankrupt. The banker then tells Lydgate that he has been considering leaving Middlemarch and transferring the management of the hospital to Dorothea, who is now a wealthy woman.

> **COMMENT:**   By leaving Middlemarch, Bulstrode hopes to avoid any scandal about his past should Raffles decide to talk.

CHAPTER SIXTY-EIGHT

On Christmas Eve, Raffles again visits Bulstrode, who has told his wife that he is "simply taking care of this wretched creature, the victim of vice, who might otherwise injure himself." He calls for a carriage for Raffles and warns him that he will pay him money only if he remains away from Middlemarch. If he returns, there will be no money for him.

Despite this uncomfortable arrangement with Raffles, Bulstrode senses that the only sure way for him to avoid a scandal is to leave Middlemarch. He asks the manager of his estate, Caleb Garth, to find a tenant for his house at Stone Court. Mr. Garth's first thought for manager of the property is Fred Vincy.

> **COMMENT:**   We can see that Mr. Garth's deeper purpose in asking Bulstrode to appoint Fred as manager at Stone Court lies in the hope that a responsible position will make Fred a reliable person, one whom his daughter could then be permitted to marry.

CHAPTER SIXTY-NINE

Caleb Garth rushes into the room where Lydgate is speaking to Mr. Bulstrode to tell him that he has found a man lying in the road. It is John Raffles; he is gravely ill and is calling for a doctor. Bulstrode is stunned; Caleb then reveals to Bulstrode that he knows of his past, because Raffles has told him. Caleb quickly offers to resign from his position as manager of Bulstrode's estate.

Lydgate examines Raffles and diagnoses his ailment as alcohol poisoning. He prescribes medicine and advises Bulstrode (who has wished for Raffles' death) that Raffles is to have no more alcohol.

Lydgate, returning home to face his own problems, sees his creditors removing some of his furniture because he has not been able to pay for it. Rosamond is noticeably shaken.

CHAPTER SEVENTY

Bulstrode is determined to keep a constant watch over Raffles so that no one other than Caleb Garth will learn about his past life. He begins to think he was hasty in his refusal of a loan to Lydgate. The doctor pays a visit to Raffles and prescribes extremely moderate doses of opium in case of sleeplessness. Before Lydgate leaves, Bulstrode presents him with a check for one thousand pounds.

> **COMMENT:** Bulstrode has quickly become obsessed with the hope of Raffles' death, although he still maintains his good intentions of keeping him alive.

At six o'clock that evening, Bulstrode begins administering small doses of opium to the restless Raffles. Later in the night, he turns the care of Raffles over to his housekeeper, Mrs. Abel. He "forgets" to tell her when the medication should stop. Raffles dies the next morning but no one questions the circumstances of his death.

> **COMMENT:** The question of Bulstrode's guilt for Raf-

fles' death is debatable. Eliot presents the act as a moral transgression rather than a legal one.

CHAPTER SEVENTY-ONE

The scene is the Green Dragon tavern, where the men of the Middlemarch meet to drink and gossip. Mr. Bambridge, the horse dealer, upon hearing of the death of Raffles, reveals his own conversation with the dead man a few days before his death. Bulstrode's secret marriage and the truth about Will Ladislaw are made known, much to the consternation of those assembled. If Raffles knew Bulstrode's secret, is it not suspicious that he died in Bulstrode's home? Is it not also true that Dr. Lydgate, who attended the deceased, has been able to clear his numerous debts within five days of the funeral?

Before long, rumors fill the town of Middlemarch. Caleb Garth tells Bulstrode that he cannot be happy working for him and resigns his position. At a meeting to discuss medical procedures to be taken against the threat of a cholera epidemic, Mr. Hawley boldly demands that Bulstrode defend himself against Raffles' allegations. Bulstrode is frightened, but angrily attacks the "proceedings" against him. Physically and emotionally distressed, he needs assistance from Lydgate when he leaves. The doctor senses that Bulstrode's gift to him probably looks to others as if it was a bribe—perhaps, he thinks, it was.

Dorothea remains loyal to Lydgate. She tells Mr. Farebrother: "You don't believe that Dr. Lydgate is guilty of anything base? I will not believe it."

BOOK EIGHT—SUNSET AND SUNRISE

CHAPTER SEVENTY-TWO

Mr. Farebrother thinks there are no grounds to open a formal investigation to prove Lydgate guiltless; he does not relish the thought of asking Lydgate directly, since he has already seen some of the doctor's pride. Dorothea is annoyed with the Reverend for his unreadiness to defend Lydgate and advances a maxim: "What do we live for, if it is not to make life less difficult for each other?"

All the townspeople who know Lydgate are anxious to prove his innocence in the matter of Raffles' death. However, the circumstances surrounding the death leave them somewhat confused and uncertain about his motives. Dorothea is firmly convinced of his innocence, but she does not wish to confront him directly about the matter. Sir James thinks, "He must act for himself." Mr. Brooke is not sure of his innocence and wishes to avoid involvement because it will cost him money. Since Bulstrode has transferred the management of the New Hospital to Dorothea and she does have certain questions to ask Lydgate about it, she sees in this an opportunity to question him indirectly about Raffles' death.

> **COMMENT:** Dorothea, an idealist like Lydgate, can readily appreciate the obstacles which beset one's plans to render service to others. Lydgate has lost both time and reputation because of his marriage to the prodigal Rosamond Vincy and the death of Raffles and the attendant guilt by association with Bulstrode.

CHAPTER SEVENTY-THREE

Lydgate himself is ready "to curse the day" he came to Middlemarch. His marriage is not the success he had hoped for; now his reputation is at stake because of Raffles and Bulstrode. He wants to clear himself but does not wish to implicate Bulstrode, especially if he is innocent, because he is now indebted to Bulstrode for the thousand pounds received the night before Raffles' death. Yet he decides to tell Rosamond nothing: "I shall do as I think right, and explain to nobody."

CHAPTER SEVENTY-FOUR

Because Middlemarch is a small town, "candor" is the vehicle used invalidly as an excuse to spread rumor. Inevitably, Rosamond Lydgate and Mrs. Bulstrode hear the stories about their husbands. Mrs. Bulstrode, who is liked and pitied by Middlemarch wives, is deeply perturbed. Rosamond, on the other hand, is more severely criticized but is still thought to be merely the victim of a marriage to a stranger and interloper, since the Vincys are of old stock and solid reputation.

Mrs. Bulstrode has believed in her husband implicitly and is shaken when Mrs. Hackbutt hints that her friends will be "loyal" to her. She is unable to obtain any information until her brother, Mr. Vincy, tells her everything he knows. Harriet Bulstrode cannot forgive her husband and judges him harshly, since she had believed the story Bulstrode told her about Raffles being a sick, helpless man whom he had befriended. Finally she confronts her husband. Both begin to cry: his confession is silent. She cannot say, "How much is only slander and false suspicion?" and he cannot say, "I am innocent."

CHAPTER SEVENTY-FIVE

Rosamond is completely involved with her own wishes and the gratification of them. She remains unchanged; she is grateful that the debts have been paid but she cannot feel any happier about the success of her marriage. She still thinks Ladislaw will eventually admire her more than Dorothea.

> **COMMENT:** Eliot observes that Rosamond is one of those women who live much in the idea that each man they meet would have preferred them if the preference had not been hopeless.

Rosamond thinks that Will would have been a more suitable

husband than Lydgate. She is happy when Lydgate receives a letter from Will stating that he will arrive in Middlemarch in a few days. Lydgate has become increasingly moody and inclined to silence. Rosamond plans a dinner party but all the invitations are declined. Her father tells her everything and then suggests that Lydgate leave town. Rosamond thinks that no one could be in a worse situation than she. Refusing to display her emotions to anyone, she also remains silent. Lydgate finally learns that Rosamond knows all, but she still says nothing. He wants her to be loyal and help him restore his reputation. But Rosamond cannot sympathize or console him about his problems because of her selfishness. Her advice is simple: "Let us go to London."

CHAPTER SEVENTY-SIX

Dorothea questions Lydgate about the management of the New Hospital. He mentions that he has been thinking of leaving Middlemarch. She takes this opportunity to beg him to tell her the truth of the Raffles matter and, at this time, he proclaims his innocence. Dorothea believes his story, then tells him that she will do all within her power to clear his name. She even offers to repay his loan from Bulstrode. Lydgate hopes he will be able to convince Rosamond that he wishes to stay in Middlemarch, at least until the townspeople believe his innocence in the matter.

CHAPTER SEVENTY-SEVEN

The following day, Dorothea pays a visit to Rosamond to explain her plans about using her money to clear Lydgate's name of any scandal. She enters the drawing room; seated with his back toward her, speaking in a low voice to Rosamond, is Will Ladislaw. Seeing Dorothea, his eyes seem "to turn to marble." Although shaken, Dorothea says in a firm voice that she has come to leave a letter for Dr. Lydgate. This "letter" is a note for one thousand pounds for Bulstrode. Indignant after her expedition, but determined to clear Dr. Lydgate, she returns to Freshitt Hall where she is still living with Celia and Sir James.

CHAPTER SEVENTY-EIGHT

Rosamond and Will stand almost paralyzed with shock from their experience. Will flies into a rage; Rosamond is in misery. He leaves, feeling that any hope of a future with Dorothea is ruined. Rosamond, still concerned with her own feelings, retires to bed. When Lydgate returns home, he finds her there, weeping hysterically. He knows that Dorothea went to visit his wife that afternoon but he has no idea of what happened, or that Dorothea never spoke to Rosamond.

> **COMMENT:** The illusions which Rosamond has carefully nurtured suddenly evaporate when Will Ladislaw angrily berates her for ruining his reputation with Dorothea.

CHAPTER SEVENTY-NINE

Lydgate does not ask Rosamond if Dorothea has called to visit, but when he sees her letter on the table in the drawing room, he knows she has been there. Will Ladislaw arrives; Lydgate tells him that Rosamond is ill. (He does not know that Will has visited earlier that day.) The topic of their conversation is the one most discussed in Middlemarch: Raffles' death. Will admits only that he has had an encounter with Raffles, but he makes no mention of Bulstrode's connection with him. When Lydgate tells Will that Dorothea is the only one who has come to his assistance, he notices a change in Will's face. Suddenly, he realizes that Dorothea is the reason for Will's return to Middlemarch. The two men are "pitying" each other, but both are very much interested in their own problems and their dim prospects for the future.

CHAPTER EIGHTY

Dorothea is invited to have dinner at Reverend Farebrother's house. She enjoys these visits because there is always something of interest to be said or done there. Farebrother is very active in his parish and performs outstanding service for his parishoners, old as well as young. Dorothea is glad to have something to do to take her mind off Will Ladislaw. When his name is mentioned during the conversation, her former anguish returns. She excuses herself on the pretense of being overtired. She cries herself to sleep and dreams of Will. She awakens in the dawn, refreshed and with her sense of the life's ideals in perspective. Dorothea again becomes concerned with the problem of Lydgate's marriage, so she decides to pay another visit to the troubled Lydgate household—to speak to Rosamond.

CHAPTER EIGHTY-ONE

On her second visit, Dorothea meets Lydgate, who mentions his wife's illness and then tells Dorothea that he has accepted her check most humbly and gratefully. Rosamond consents to see Dorothea, but is at a loss as to the purpose of Mrs. Casaubon's visit. She feels inferior to Dorothea, who is Lydgate's benefactor and Ladislaw's idol; she feels that Dorothea will parade her advantage before her.

Their meeting becomes emotional. Dorothea's heart goes out to the helplessness of Rosamond, who has become aware that she has misjudged Dorothea's motives. Dorothea explains to Rosamond that she had come the previous day to tell her of her plans to clear Lydgate's name. Dorothea passionately pleads Lydgate's innocence. Rosamond begins to cry hysterically when Dorothea says to her, "How can we live and think that anyone has trouble—piercing trouble—and we could help them, and never try?" She then gently chides Rosamond for not allowing her husband to be open with her. She then gives her ideas on marriage, but becomes too emotional to finish. Rosamond, guessing the reason for her emotion to be her thoughts of Ladislaw, tells Dorothea that she was mistaken about what she saw yesterday. Rosamond explains that Will was actually declaring his love for Dorothea and rebuffing hers.

> **COMMENT:**   When her artifice and self-possession are forgotten, Rosamond is capable of genuine feeling. By admitting her failure to captivate Will Ladislaw she has renewed Dorothea's trust in her character.

CHAPTER EIGHTY-TWO

Will thinks he has no choice now but to leave Middlemarch

again. His primary reason for returning had been to see Dorothea; now he feels that she will have nothing to do with him. On a visit to the Lydgate household, Rosamond slips Will a note at tea which tells him that she has explained the situation to Dorothea. Exhilarated at this news, Will hopes for a reconciliation with Dorothea.

CHAPTER EIGHTY-THREE

Dorothea is relieved after her conversation with Rosamond. On the second morning after her visit, Miss Henrietta Noble, an aunt of Reverend Farebrother, pays a visit to her at the request of Will Ladislaw. She says Will fears he has offended her and asks if he may see her for a few minutes. Dorothea agrees. When Will arrives, she tells him she is "glad" he came. They stand silently at first but finally they confess their love for one another. He tells her that he cannot marry her because of Casaubon's will, which stipulates that she will lose the remaining money if they marry. She tells him that she hates her wealth, but her heart will break if he leaves. They decide to marry within three weeks.

> **COMMENT:** Dorothea is independently wealthy, aside from her inheritance of Casaubon's estate.

CHAPTER EIGHTY-FOUR

The Reform Bill has been defeated in the House of Lords and Reverend Cadwallader, who favored the creation of peers to push through the bill, is discussing the political ramifications of the day with the Chettams and Mrs. Cadwallader on the lawn of Freshitt Hall. Mr. Brooke approaches dejectedly. He reveals the news of Dorothea's intended marriage to Ladislaw. Sir James turns white with rage; "I should have called him out and shot him," he cries. Reverend Cadwallader addresses Sir James, "My dear fellow, we are rather apt to consider an act wrong because it is unpleasant to us." Mr. Brooke decides not to think evil of Will until he hears good reason for doing so. He thinks of him in terms of a "son," inheriting Tipton and Freshitt. Mrs. Cadwallader remarks that "his blood is a frightful mixture."

Celia goes to her sister to advise her against the marriage. Dorothea tells Celia she is going to London; after much discussion, Celia realizes that nothing will change her sister's decision to marry Will. She fears that she will never see Dorothea again, since Sir James will not visit London because of his hatred for Will Ladislaw.

CHAPTER EIGHTY-FIVE

Bulstrode still has not made a full confession of his past life to his wife. He decides that some day (when he is dying) he will "tell her all." Mrs. Bulstrode suggests that they make amends to the Lydgates, who are also leaving Middlemarch. Bulstrode knows, however, that the doctor will not accept anything from him. Mrs. Bulstrode also advises him to make Fred Vincy the manager of the property at Stone Court. (Caleb Garth had resigned after Raffles told him of Mr. Bulstrode's past.)

CHAPTER EIGHTY-SIX

Caleb Garth learns of Mr. Bulstrode's plan to make Fred Vincy the manager of Stone Court. He wants to be the first to tell his daughter Mary. She is sitting in the garden. He casually begins a conversation about Fred; although she admits her love for him, she observes, "We must wait for each other a long while." When he tells her the news, she is filled with joy and rushes to tell Fred, who is coming to the garden to visit her. Fred is surprised and delighted. He and Mary sit in the garden for a long time to discuss their future.

>   **COMMENT:** The novel ends at this chapter. However, because Eliot knew her readers would like to know "how everything worked out" for her characters, she adds a Finale, or final chapter of explanation.

FINALE

Mary and Fred Vincy had both a happy and successful marriage. He became a theoretical and practical farmer and won the admiration of the people of Middlemarch. They had three sons to bless their marriage.

Dr. Lydgate gained an excellent practice in the area surrounding London. He and Rosamond "adjusted" to one another, each accepting the strong and weak points of the other's personality. He was a successful man (although he considered himself a failure), and died at fifty, leaving Rosamond and their four children. Later, she married an elderly and wealthy physician.

Dorothea and Will were still bound together by their strong love. She never repented that she had given up her wealth for her marriage to Will. He continued to work for the reforms which he had begun when he was a youth.

Mr. Brooke continued to correspond with Dorothea and Will and invited them to the Grange. Dorothea wrote Celia of the news that she had a son. Sir James finally relented, visiting them so that Celia could see the child. In this way a reconciliation was brought about between the two families. Mr. Brooke lived to a ripe old age and Dorothea's son inherited his estate.

Sir James, however, always regarded Dorothea's marriage as a mistake. He disliked Will, but never showed it openly for Celia's sake. The feeling was reciprocated on Will's part.

Those who did not know Dorothea usually thought she could not have been "a nice woman" because she married a much older man and then, a year after his death, threw away her inheritance and married a man young enough to be her first husband's son. Dorothea, however, led an important if obscure life; her good acts had a diffused effect on those around her. "The growing of good in the world is partly dependent on unhistoric acts." Our life is not as bad for us as it might have been, owing to the number of people like Dorothea who led hidden lives and who rest in "unvisited tombs."

CHARACTER ANALYSIS

DOROTHEA BROOKE (later Mrs. Casaubon, Mrs. Ladislaw):
The idealistic and intelligent "heroine" of the novel, whose character and high values enable her to surmount the difficulties which her disappointing first marriage brings. Her second marriage is to Will Ladislaw; unlike the first, it is happy since it is based on a realistic appraisal of her husband's personality and career. "Her mind was theoretic, and yearned by its nature after some lofty conception of the world which might frankly include the parish of Tipton and her own rule of conduct there; she was enamoured of intensity and greatness, and rash in embracing whatever seemed to her to have those aspects; likely to seek martyrdom, to make retractions, and then to incur martyrdom after all in a quarter where she had not sought it" (Book 1, Chapter 1).

CELIA BROOKE: The younger sister of Dorothea. Less intense than her sister, she marries Sir James Chettam, who had originally courted her sister. "The rural opinion about the new young ladies, even among the cottagers, was generally in favor of Celia, as being so amiable and innocent-looking, while Miss Brooke's large eyes seemed, like her religion, too unusual and striking. Poor Dorothea! Compared with her, the innocent-looking Celia was knowing and worldly-wise" (Book 1, Chapter 1).

MR. ARTHUR BROOKE: The uncle of Dorothea and Celia, a sturdy English squire. "Their uncle, a man nearly sixty, of acquiescent temper, miscellaneous opinions, and uncertain vote. He had traveled in his younger years, and was held in this part of the county to have contracted a too rambling habit of mind. Mr. Brooke's conclusions were as difficult to predict as the weather: it was only safe to say that he would act with benevolent intentions, and that he would spend as little money as possible in carrying them out" (Book 1, Chapter 1).

REV. EDWARD CASAUBON: A pedantic scholar who marries Dorothea because he sees in her a companion and secretary. "I feed too much on the inward sources; I live too much with the dead. My mind is something like the ghost of an ancient, wandering about the world and trying mentally to construct it as it used to be, in spite of ruin and confusing changes" (Book 1, Chapter 1).

WILL LADISLAW: The young, handsome relative of Mr. Casaubon whose artistic and literary skills make him suspect to the people of Middlemarch. He becomes editor of the town newspaper. "Genius, he held, is necessarily intolerant of fetters: on the one hand it must have the utmost play for its spontaneity; on the other, it may confidently await those messages from the universe which summon it to its peculiar work, only placing itself in an attitude of receptivity towards all sublime chances. The attitudes of receptivity are various, and Will had sincerely tried many of them" (Book 1, Chapter 10).

DR. TERTIUS LYDGATE: The "hero" of the novel is a medical man whose ideals and visionary plans are dimmed by the reality of a marriage to the selfish Rosamond Vincy. "He was but seven-and-twenty, an age at which many men are not quite common— at which they are hopeful of achievement, resolute in avoidance, thinking that Mammon shall never put a bit in their mouths and get astride their backs, but rather that Mammon, if they have anything to do with him, shall draw their chariot . . ." (Book 2, Chapter 15). "He carried to his studies in London, Edinburgh, and Paris, the conviction that the medical profession as it might be was the finest in the world; presenting the most perfect inter-change between science and art; offering the most direct alliance between intellectual conquest and the social good" (Book 2, Chapter 15).

ROSAMOND VINCY: The beautiful, egotistical, and unrealistic daughter of the mayor of Middlemarch; the debutante who becomes the wife of Dr. Lydgate. "She judged of her own symptoms as those of awakening love, and she held it still more natural that Mr. Lydgate should have fallen in love at first sight of her. These things happened so often at balls, and why not by the morning light, when the complexion showed all the better for it? . . . And here was Mr. Lydgate suddenly corresponding to her ideal, being altogether foreign to Middlemarch, carrying a certain air of distinction congruous with good family, and possessing connections which offered vistas of that middle-class heaven, rank: a man of talent, also, whom it would be especially delightful to enslave" (Book 1, Chapter 12).

FRED VINCY: Rosamond's young, careless brother whose debts and lack of purpose prevent him from marrying his love, Mary Garth.

MARY GARTH: The plain and practical daughter of the estate agent, Caleb Garth, who insists that Fred Vincy prove his stability before their marriage.

MR. VINCY: The ambitious mayor of Middlemarch, whose indulgent attitude towards his son abruptly ends when Fred fails to receive a legacy from Peter Featherstone, his uncle.

MRS. VINCY: Mother of Fred and Rosamond, she reflects an intense enjoyment of life, which may account for Fred's lack of direction and Rosamond's liberality.

CALEB GARTH: The industrious, respectable, and charitable estate manager who often lends his time, skill, and money to others, even at the subsequent expense of his own family.

NICHOLAS BULSTRODE: A strong, influential banker who suddenly discovers that his past life may be revealed and his reputation in Middlemarch destroyed.

JOHN RAFFLES: The coarse, unscrupulous stranger who uses his knowledge of Will Ladislaw's and Mr. Bulstrode's pasts to make money by blackmailing Bulstrode. His subsequent death leads to a crisis in the lives of Bulstrode and Dr. Lydgate.

JOSHUA RIGG: The "frog-faced" man who becomes the heir to the land and fortune of Peter Featherstone; he is his natural son.

PETER FEATHERSTONE: The ailing, suspicious, and ill-tempered owner of Stone Court, a wealthy estate. The first of his two wives was a Garth; the second, a sister of Mrs. Vincy. His expected death leads to speculation about his legacy and becomes a focal point of interest in Middlemarch.

REVEREND CAMDEN FAREBROTHER: The amiable and gifted vicar of St. Botolph's, who amends his minor vices when given the chance to assume the post of vicar of Lowick.

MRS. CADWALLADER: The wife of the rector of the parishes of Tipton and Freshitt, she is a lively hearer and teller of Middlemarch rumor. Of "immeasurably" high birth, she is not above stooping to matchmaking.

SIR JAMES CHETTAM: The rejected suitor of Dorothea Brooke who finds a full and happy life when he marries her younger sister Celia.

CRITICAL COMMENTARY

SENSE OF ORGANIC WHOLE AND SKILL IN PLOT: The attitude of many critics in the twentieth century to Victorian literature has been a mixture of indifference and contempt because of the marked impact of Freudian and Jungian psychological theory, the watersheds of two world wars, and the influence of Marxist philosophy. Yet for those who actually read the works of Dickens, Thackeray, and their contemporaries, the experience is rewarding. Apart from other considerations, these novelists and, in particular, George Eliot, were accomplished storytellers. Narrative, even in the stream-of-consciousness technique, involves incident; the mode and quality of the action create the interest, suspense, and surprise which characterize successful fiction. And here, in plot, is precisely where one finds the key to success in Eliot's novels. As Lord David Cecil has observed in *Early Victorian Novelists:* "It is very rare for a Victorian novelist before George Eliot to conceive the story as an organic whole of which every incident and character forms a contributory and integral part." The realistic quality of major incidents places no excessive burden upon the reader's credulity. Since what happens is probable, our suspension of disbelief is not impaired, for the motives and events which are presented to us in the action are justifiable and logical within the story's realm.

PERCEPTION OF PROVINCIAL ATTITUDES: Although George Eliot's technical skill is, perhaps, related chiefly to structural aspects, understanding and unraveling basic motivations found in human action are vital to her work. Claude Bisell (ELH, VIII) suggests that "George Eliot is at her strongest and best working in a social setting that she thoroughly understands and exploring a complicated network of motives with assurance and precision." The tracing of the thought of a character before he acts is a favorite interest of Eliot. The elaborate thought labyrinths of Henry James's characters are found only in Eliot's "aristocratic" characters (of whom there are relatively few in her novels). She is most accomplished, however, in explication of the thinking of the types that she understood best: the sturdy, respectable middle class and less complex lower classes of the era in which she lived. Years of extended observation and experience in Warwickshire and Coventry with the kind of people who inhabit her novels are reflected continually. Her preference is for unobtrusive picturing of the details of a character's thinking. Her use of the dramatic is very sparing and effective; it is employed primarily in scenes of conflict, such as those in which Dr. Lydgate and Rosamond or Raffles and Bulstrode engage.

PICTORIAL POWER MORE THAN DRAMATIC: Discussing the need for the dramatic in *The Craft of Fiction,* Percy Lubbock has noted: "Inevitably as the plot thickens and the climax approaches—inevitably, whenever an impression is to be emphasized and driven home—narration gives place to enactment. . . . Most novelists, I think, seem to betray, like Thackeray, a preference for one method or the other, for picture or for drama; one sees in a moment how Fielding, Balzac, George Eliot incline to the first, in their diverse manners, and Tolstoy (certainly Tolstoy, in spite of his big range) or Dostoevsky to the second, the scenic way."

PROBABLE INFLUENCE OF BALZAC: The view that Eliot may have been influenced in her style by Balzac is perhaps valid since in an essay which appeared in *The Leader* for July 21, 1855 called "The Morality of Wilhelm Meister" she eulogized Balzac as "perhaps the most wonderful writer of fiction the world has ever seen." That she could hardly have permitted herself to imitate his naturalism, however, is forcefully underlined by her comment in the same article "he drags us by his magic force through scene after scene of unmitigated vice, till the effect of walking among the human carrion is a moral nausea."

ELIOT COMPARED WITH TOLSTOY: From the English critic F. R. Leavis [*The Great Tradition* (London, 1948), pp. 124–125)] comes the strong statement of Eliot's superiority over the later Victorian novelists and a comparison of Eliot with Leo Tolstoy, the author of *War and Peace:* "I affirm my conviction that, by the side of George Eliot—and the comparison shouldn't be necessary—Meredith appears as a shallow exhibitionist . . . and Hardy, decent as he is, as a provincial manufacturer of gauche and heavy fictions that sometimes have corresponding value. For a positive indication of her place and quality, I think of a Russian, not Turgenev, but a far greater, Tolstoy—who, we all know, is pre-eminent in getting the 'spirit of life itself.' George Eliot, of course, is not so transcendentally great as Tolstoy, but she *is* great, and great in the same way. . . . Of George Eliot it can be said that her best work has a Tolstoyan depth and reality."

RATIONALISM AS HER "RELIGION": Eliot's religious belief or lack of it is a topic which has brought forth divergent critical interpretations of her novels and correspondence. In his book *Nineteenth Century Studies,* Basil Willey, the respected English critic and scholar, disagrees with Lord David Cecil's view that George Eliot was "not religious." Willey fails to see why this expression is used by Cecil: "Religious," Willey states, "seems to me to be just what she was and many others of whom she is the type; the whole predicament she represents was that of the religious temperament cut off . . . from the traditional objects of veneration, and the traditional intellectual formulations." Although Eliot was not a "practicing Christian," Willey suggests that she knew "the hunger and thirst" for just living and the need for self-control and renunciation, "the need to lose one's life in order to gain it."

Jerome Thale, in *The Novels of George Eliot,* views the route of the Victorian intellectual—"extending from earnest belief through disbelief to a new, often secular, faith. As psychologist and as student of the new theology, George Eliot saw religion as valid subjectively rather than objectively. For her, our creeds, our notions of God, are true not as facts but as symbols, as expressions of states of mind. Faith is good as disbelief is bad, not because a God exists but because they are symptoms of a healthy state of consciousness. The novel does not give statements as explicit as this, but that is surely the inference to be made from the action."

A strikingly personal revelation of her view of man's need for religious belief occurs in a letter to Mme. Bodichon on November 26, 1862. "Pray don't ever ask me again not to rob a man of his religious belief, as if you thought my mind tended to such a robbery. I have too profound a conviction of the efficacy that lies in all sincere faith, and the spiritual blight that comes with no faith, to have any negative propagandism in me. In fact, I have very little sympathy with Freethinkers as a class, and have lost all interest in mere antagonism to religious doctrines. I care only to know, if possible, the lasting meaning that lies in all religious doctrine from the beginning till now."

ELIOT LETTERS ABOUT *MIDDLEMARCH*:   December 1, 1871. "This day the first part of "Middlemarch" was published. I ought by this time to have finished the fourth part, but an illness which began soon after our return from Haslemere has robbed me of two months."

December 20 (*Journal*). "My health has become very troublesome during the last three weeks, and I can get on but tardily. Even now I am but on p. 227 on my fourth part."

January 29, 1872 (*Journal*). "It is now the last day but one of January. I have finished the fourth part—i.e., the second volume—of *Middlemarch*. The first part, published on December 1, has been excellently well received; and the second part will be published the day after to-morrow."

February 21, 1872 (Letter). "It has caused me some uneasiness that the third part is two sheets less than the first. But Mr. Lewes insisted that the death of old Featherstone was the right point to pause at; and he cites your approbation of the part as a proof that effectiveness is secured in spite of diminished quantity."

September 13, 1872 (Letter). "*Middlemarch* is done—all except a small finale, which I prefer reserving a little. The rest I hope to see the last little proof of at the beginning of next week."

November 4, 1872 (Letter). "I have finished my book [*Middlemarch*], and am thoroughly at peace about it—not because I am convinced of its perfection, but because I have lived to give out what it was in me to give, and have not been hindered by illness or death from making my work a whole, such as it is."

November 22, 1872 (Letter). "Expect to be immensely disappointed with the close of *Middlemarch*. But look back to the Prelude."

December 1, 1872 (Letter). ". . . *Maga*'s [*Blackwood Magazine's*] review of *Middlemarch*. I have just now been reading the review myself—Mr. Lewes had meant at first to follow his rule of not allowing me to see what is written about myself—and I am pleased to find the right moral note struck everywhere, both in remark and quotation. Especially I am pleased with the writer's sensibility to the pathos in Mr. Casaubon's character and position, and with the discernment he shows about Bulstrode. But it is a perilous matter to approve the praise which is given to our own matters."

ELIOT'S REPUTATION BASED ON HER PSYCHOLOGICAL INSIGHT: Because of the advances made in fiction techniques, and new scientific knowledge of the human psyche, the twentieth-century novelist has at his disposal much direction which George Eliot did not receive. Because their hasty and dilletante tastes prevent many readers and critics from even reading her novels (one supposes because of the didacticism of occasional chapters and a mistaken view that stereotyped sentimentality drips from every page), the real nature of her style and value remains relatively unknown to the general reading public.

Eliot's brilliant psychological penetration was one of the English models for which Proust admitted great admiration. The quality novels of Woolf, Joyce, and Faulkner and a handful of European novelists represent the best, in terms of technical advances and plumbing of the mind, that the twentieth century has produced. For her time, George Eliot's contributions both for virtuosity in form and in psychological depth are unmatched in English fiction.

ESSAY QUESTIONS AND ANSWERS

1. Who are the major characters in *Middlemarch* and what do they represent?

ANSWER: The most important portraits in this extensive gallery of English life are those of two idealistic people: Dorothea Brooke (Mrs. Casaubon) and Dr. Tertius Lydgate. Both are intelligent, scrupulous, and dedicated to the task of improving the lot of their fellow men. He wishes to succeed in a far-reaching experiment and to broaden the effectiveness of the country hospital. She is concerned with improving the living conditions of poorer working classes by advocating the construction of modest cottages. Both visionaries, however, quickly find that ideas and ideals are, in themselves, no assurance of success. The way of the world is strong; complex obstacles appear to obstruct the best-intentioned plans. Human avarice, pettiness, or plain perverseness block progress. At times, their own romantic or injudicious decisions make progress difficult. The marriages of Dorothea (her first) and Lydgate push them farther away from their broad humanitarian goals. Perhaps, then, a chief concern of the novel is to present two thoughtful, sensitive, but fallible people who are forced continually to sustain their strength in the realities of living.

Other characters in the novel represent various levels of English society at the time of the Reform Bill: Sir James Chettam and Mr. Brooke are typical of the wealthy, landed gentry; among the clergy Reverend Casaubon and Reverend Cadwallader are clearly a few rungs higher on social and economic ladders than Mr. Farebrother; Mr. Vincy and Mr. Bulstrode are, respectively, the mayor and the banker of Middlemarch, positions which give their families the opportunities for educational and cultural pursuits denied the less prosperous working families such as Caleb Garth's. Even on the lower social levels Eliot makes distinctions in rank among Trumbull the auctioneer, Bambridge the horse dealer, and dozens of minor characters who help to give the novel its panoramic effects.

2. Why is *Middlemarch* considered one of George Eliot's best novels?

ANSWER: The book is representative of the most significant contributions which George Eliot made in English literature and in the development of the novel. First, it presents a vivid and accurate panorama of English life in the third decade of the nineteenth century. Readers such as William Wordsworth agreed that the pictures of rural people were authentic; from the wealthier class of squires and managers, down through the middle-class pictures of clergymen and professionals, to the simple farmers and journeymen, there is an unmistakable truth in her description and psychology. Her scenes of provincial life: the horse fair, the auction, the political rally, the hospital board meeting, the tavern gossip, the talk of workingmen, doctors, and clergy—all help to recreate an era with authentic color and movement.

Secondly, the complexity of the plot interests the reader consistently; skillful suspension of decision, which many characters face, stimulates curiosity; the abrupt revelation of sudden or hidden incidents creates surprise and intensifies interest. Some of the chief decisions made early in the novel include:

1. Dorothea Brooke's acceptance of Rev. Casaubon's marriage proposal.

2. Lydgate's choice of Rosamond as a wife.

3. Peter Featherstone's changing of his will.

4. Lydgate's vote for Mr. Tyke.

Thirdly, a mastery of deftness in characterization makes the reader interested in the future of most of the characters. Rarely are we unable to perceive a distinct human being made unique through specific details of speech, outlook, or action. Eliot's gifted insight into human motivation is apparent throughout; the characters act according to their natures after consideration of their choices: both Dorothea Brooke and John Raffles, for example, act the way we are led to believe they will act. The effective use of dialogue, suggestive imagery, autobiographical, ethical, and technical considerations also contribute to make *Middlemarch* a most valuable and artistic novel.

3. Why is the book called "a novel about marriage?"

ANSWER: As in any novel, each of the four plots in *Middlemarch* is concerned with the problems which people face either because of circumstances or their own injudicious acts. Much of the action in each plot, however, is concerned with marriage difficulties.

a. Dorothea Brooke has romantically imagined marriage to Casaubon as a chance for her to fulfill an ambition to serve a great man in his work. Her illusions disappear, however, within a few weeks; even on her honeymoon in Rome she must face the sobering reality that her scholar husband married her for practical purposes, and is incapable of responding to her "ardent" nature. That she decides to remain loyal to him in spite of his shortcomings is, unquestionably, a difficult—even a noble—choice for her to make, considering how little joy she expects to receive in return from Casaubon.

b. Dr. Lydgate and Rosamond Vincy, like Dorothea Brooke and the Reverend Casaubon, have married for the wrong reasons. Rosamond's "theory" of love is that proximity breeds love; since Dr. Lydgate has to visit the Vincy household frequently owing to her brother Fred's illness, Rosamond presumes that they have fallen in love. To her, Lydgate fulfills her superficial requirements for marriage: he has the education, position, manners, dress, and voice she admires; in other words, all the external necessities needed to fulfill her concept of "husband." Indifferent and unconcerned about Lydgate's ideals, she later creates a burden of debt for him through her excessive and irresponsible spending. Lydgate, who had viewed his relationship with Rosamond merely as a harmless flirtation not to be taken seriously (because of his career plans), is moved by her tears; the sight of this single display of genuine emotion prompts him to ask for her hand. His life with Rosamond will be devoid of research and full of regret.

c. Mr. Bulstrode the banker and his wife Harriet have led a life together in which the real character of Bulstrode and his unscrupulous past have been concealed. His hypocrisy is finally revealed after the death of John Raffles.

d. Mary Garth finds herself unable to accept Fred Vincy as a husband because of his careless, uncertain future. Unsure of a career and given to incurring gambling debts, Fred is able, finally, to correct his debilitating habits and to win her. Mary's common sense and realistic values prevent her from consenting to a marriage which promises little security. Unlike the other characters in the novel, who marry not for love but for some romantically specious reason, Mary is in love with Fred but refuses to risk union with him until she can be assured that he is capable of providing for a family.

4. How is the term "The Wise Woman" used in reference to the novel?

ANSWER: George Eliot, like many Victorian novelists, often interrupts her story to comment on the significance of a character's thought or action. These omniscient observations are recognized by most critics as an explanatory or didactic technique, one not unlike the chanting of a chorus in Greek drama. The phrase "The Wise Woman" refers then, to the voice of the author. It is usually heard at the end of the chapter. Critics F. R. Leavis and Quentin Anderson agree in their detection of a personal tone in Eliot's comparison of Dorothea to a saint. In the Prelude Eliot says: "Here and there is born a Saint Theresa, foundress of nothing, whose loving heartbeats and sobs after an unattained goodness tremble off and are dispersed among hindrances, instead of centering in some long recognizable deed." Whether Eliot's comments enhance the novel's art or not is a choice left to the reader's judgment.

5. What are the dominant images in the novel?

ANSWER: By using carefully chosen imagery Eliot has intensified emotional aspects of characters and given insights into the planning of her novel's structure. Casaubon's life, for example, is usually described in terms of small, confining places. His rooms are dark, stuffy, and old. He reveals in one of his first speeches that he keeps part of his research materials in "pigeon-holes." He is reminiscent of a "specimen from a mine" or "a description above the door of a museum."

The novel is a complex one, and Eliot has been required to

weave together strands of several plots, each of which contains characters whose lives intersect with others. As Professor Gordon S. Haight has pointed out, there are numerous images of weaving, binding, and linking in *Middlemarch:* "Some of them refer to Lydgate and Rosamond. Lydgate has set out to discover the tissue common to all living matter, taking up the thread of his investigations or adding links to the chain of scientific evidence; but he is caught in the gossamer web of love, and his life is bound into one with Rosamond's. From the beginning she has woven a little future for herself. When she lays aside her reticule she is seldom without a thread in her hand for lace-making or tatting."

BIBLIOGRAPHY

The complete *Works* of George Eliot has been published in twenty-five volumes (Warwickshire edition, 1908). Following is a list of titles under two general topics. Plentiful material concerning *Middlemarch* may be found in the works listed.

LETTERS

Haight, G. S. (ed.) *The George Eliot Letters*. 7 vols. 1954–55.

BIOGRAPHY

Bullett, Gerald. *George Eliot: Her Life and Books*. 1947.

Cross, J. W. *George Eliot's Life as Related in Her Letters and Journals*. 3 vols. 1885.

Haldane, E. S. *George Eliot and Her Times*. 1927.

Hanson, L., and E. M. Hanson. *Marian Evans and George Eliot*. 1952.

May, J. Lewis. *George Eliot: A Study*. 1930.

Stevens, George. *George Eliot*. 1902.

Williams, Blanche C. *George Eliot: A Biography*. 1936.

CRITICISM

Bennett, Joan. *George Eliot: Her Mind and Art*. 1954. Paperback.

Hardy, Barbara. *The Novels of George Eliot*. 1959.

Harvey, W. J. *The Art of George Eliot*. 1961.

Stump, Reva. *Movement and Vision in George Eliot's Novels.* 1959.

Thale, Jerome. *The Novels of George Eliot.* 1959.

INDIVIDUAL CHAPTERS OF CRITICISM

Baker, Ernest. *The English Novel.* Vols. III, IV. 1930, 1934.

Baugh, Albert C. and others. *A Literary History of England.* 1948.

Cecil, Lord David. *Early Victorian Novelists.* 1935.

Holloway, John. *The Victorian Sage.* 1953. Paperback.

Leavis, F. R. *The Great Tradition.* 1948. Paperback.

Lubbock, Percy. *The Craft of Fiction.* 1921. Paperback.

Willey, Basil. *Nineteenth Century Studies.* 1949.

Woolf, Virginia. *The Common Reader.* 1925. Paperback.

Stevenson, Lionel. *The English Novel.* 1960. Paperback.

NOTES

NOTES

NOTES

NOTES

NOTES

NOTES

NOTES

NOTES

ACHEBE - Things Fall Apart
AESCHYLUS - The Plays
ALBEE - Who's Afraid of Virginia Woolf
AQUINAS, ST. THOMAS - The Philosophy
ARISTOPHANES - The Plays
ARISTOTLE - The Philosophy
AUGUSTINE, ST. - The Works
AUSTEN - Emma/Mansfield Park
AUSTEN - Pride and Prejudice
BECKETT - Waiting for Godot
Beowulf
BRADBURY- The Martian Chronicles
BRECHT - The Plays
BRONTE - Jane Eyre
BRONTE - Wuthering Heights
BUCK - The Good Earth
CAMUS - The Stranger
CATHER - My Antonia
CERVANTES - Don Quixote
CHAUCER - Canterbury Tales
CHEKHOV - The Plays
CHOPIN - The Awakening
COLERIDGE - Rime of the Ancient Mariner
CONRAD - Heart of Darkness/Secret Sharer
CONRAD - Lord Jim
COOPER - Last of the Mohicans
CRANE - Red Badge of Courage
DANTE - The Divine Comedy
DE BEAUVOIR- Second Sex
DEFOE - Robinson Crusoe
DESCARTES - The Philosophy
DICKENS - Bleak House
DICKENS - David Copperfield
DICKENS - Great Expectations
DICKENS - Hard Times
DICKENS - Oliver Twist
DICKENS - A Tale of Two Cities
DICKINSON - The Poetry
DINESEN - Out of Africa
DOCTOROW- Ragtime
DONNE - The Poetry & The Metaphysical Poets
DOSTOYEVSKY - Brothers Karamazov
DREISER - Sister Carrie
ELIOT - Middlemarch
ELIOT - Silas Marner
ELIOT - Murder in the Cathedral & Poems
ELIOT - Waste Land
ELLISON - Invisible Man
EMERSON - Writings
EURIPIDES, AESCHYLUS, ARISTOPHANES - The Plays
EURIPIDES - The Plays

FAULKNER - Absalom, Absalom!
FAULKNER - As I Lay Dying
FAULKNER - Light in August
FAULKNER - Sound and the Fury
FIELDING - Joseph Andrews
FIELDING - Tom Jones
FITZGERALD - The Great Gatsby
FITZGERALD - Tender is the Night
FLAUBERT - Madame Bovary/Three Tales
FORSTER - Passage to India/Howard's End
FRANK - Diary of a Young Girl
FREUD - Interpretation of Dreams
FROST - The Poetry
GARCIA-MARQUEZ - One Hundred Years of Solitude
GOETHE - Faust
GOLDING - Lord of the Flies
Greek and Roman Classics
Greek and Roman Classics
GREENE - Major Works
HAMMETT - The Maltese Falcon/Thin Man
HARDY - Far from the Madding Crowd
HARDY - The Mayor of Casterbridge
HARDY - Return of the Native
HARDY - Tess of the D'Urbervilles
HAWTHORNE - House of the Seven Gables/ Marble Faun
HAWTHORNE - The Scarlett Letter
HELLER - Catch-22
HEMINGWAY- A Farewell to Arms
HEMINGWAY - For Whom the Bell Tolls
HEMINGWAY - Major Works
HEMINGWAY - The Old Man and the Sea
HEMINGWAY - The Snows of Kilimanjaro
HEMINGWAY - The Sun Also Rises
HESSE - Siddhartha
HOMER - The Iliad
HOMER - The Odyssey
HUGO - Les Miserables
HUXLEY - Major Works
IBSEN - The Plays
JAMES - Portrait of a Lady
JAMES - The Turn of the Screw
JAMES - Washington Square
JOYCE - Portrait of the Artist as a Young Man
KAFKA - Major Works
KEATS - The Poetry
KESEY - One Flew Over the Cuckoo's Nest
KNOWLES - A Separate Peace
LAWRENCE - Sons & Lovers
LEE - To Kill a Mockingbird
LEGUIN - Left Hand of Darkness
LEWIS - Babbitt
LOCKE & HOBBES - The Philosophies

(Continued)

(Continued)

LONDON - Call of the Wild
MACHIAVELLI - The Prince
MARLOWE - Dr. Faustus
Marxist & Utopian Socialists
MELVILLE - Billy Budd
MELVILLE - Moby Dick
MILLER - The Crucible/A View from the Bridge
MILLER - Death of a Salesman
MILTON - Paradise Lost
MOLIERE - The Plays
MORE - Utopia
MORRISON - Beloved
Mythology
The New Testament
The New Testament
NIETZSCHE - The Philosophy
The Old Testament as Living Literature
O'NEILL - Desire Under the Elms
O'NEILL - Long Day's Journey into Night
O'NEILL - The Plays
ORWELL - Animal Farm
ORWELL - 1984
PATON - Cry the Beloved Country
PLATO - The Republic and Selected Dialogues
POE - Tales and Poems
POPE - Rape of the Lock & Poems
RAWLINGS - The Yearling
REMARQUE - All Quiet on the Western Front
Rousseau & the 18th Century Philosophers
SALINGER - Catcher in the Rye
SALINGER - Franny & Zooey
SARTRE - No Exit/The Flies

SHAKESPEARE - Antony and Cleopatra
SHAKESPEARE - As You Like It
SHAKESPEARE - Hamlet
SHAKESPEARE - Henry IV, Part 1
SHAKESPEARE - Henry IV, Part 2
SHAKESPEARE - Henry V
SHAKESPEARE - Julius Caesar
SHAKESPEARE - King Lear
SHAKESPEARE - Macbeth
SHAKESPEARE - The Merchant of Venice
SHAKESPEARE - A Midsummer Night's Dream
SHAKESPEARE - Othello
SHAKESPEARE - Richard II
SHAKESPEARE - Richard III
SHAKESPEARE - Romeo and Juliet

SHAKESPEARE - Selected Comedies
SHAKESPEARE - Sonnets
SHAKESPEARE - Taming of the Shrew
SHAKESPEARE - Tempest
SHAKESPEARE - Winter's Tale
SHAKESPEARE - Twelfth Night

SHAW - Major Plays
SHAW - Pygmalion
SHAW - Saint Joan
SINCLAIR - The Jungle
Sir Gawain and the Green Knight
SKINNER - Walden Two
SOLZHENITSYN - One Day in the Life of Ivan Denisovich
SOPHOCLES - The Plays
SPENSER - The Faerie Queene
STEINBECK - The Grapes of Wrath
STEINBECK - Major Works
STEINBECK - Of Mice and Men
STEINBECK - The Pearl/Red Pony
SWIFT - Gulliver's Travels
THACKERAY - Vanity Fair/Henry Esmond
THOREAU - Walden
TOLKEIN - Fellowship of the Ring
TOLSTOY - War and Peace
TURGENEV - Fathers and Sons
TWAIN - Huckleberry Finn
TWAIN - Tom Sawyer
UPDIKE - Rabbit Run/Rabbit Redux
VIRGIL - Aeneid
VOLTAIRE - Candide/The Philosophies
VONNEGUT - Slaughterhouse Five
WALKER - The Color Purple
WARREN - All the King's Men
WAUGH - Major Works
WELLS - Invisible Man/War of the Worlds
WHARTON - Ethan Frome
WHITMAN - Leaves of Grass
WILDE - The Plays
WILDER - Our Town/Bridge of San Luis Rey
WILLIAMS - The Glass Menagerie
WILLIAMS - Major Plays
WILLIAMS - A Streetcar Named Desire
WOLFE - Look Homeward, Angel/Of Time and the River
WOOLF - Mrs. Dalloway/To the Lighthouse
WORDSWORTH - The Poetry
WRIGHT - Native Son
YEATS - The Poetry
ZOLA - Germinal

PRENTICE HALL